PRAISE FOR *SURVIVING ADOLESCENCE*

"If you have ever worked with adolescents, tried to raise them, or simply reflected on adolescent behavior in this day and time, read this work by Michael Gilbert. He is a former teacher, higher educator, parent, and consummate observer of human nature. Not only is the book insightful, the key discussion points listed at the end of each chapter are worth rereading and potentially posting for consultation when and if any questions about adolescent behaviors, personality traits, or perspectives cause tension or dissension within your home or, for educators, within your classrooms. The book is strengthened not only by experience but also by a robust understanding of ways to work with individuals with different personalities, based on their needs, concerns, and receptiveness to guidance, advice, or correction. When the moment comes to send burgeoning adults on to the next steps in their lives, the lessons that can be gleaned from *Surviving Adolescence* will be of great value not only to the parent or educator but also to the adolescents who are transitioning into adulthood under your aegis."

—Angela M. Sewall, dean emerita, College of Education, University of Arkansas, Little Rock

"Anyone who has or may have any dealings with an adolescent child needs this book! Dr. Michael Gilbert shares his considerable professional and personal wisdom to unlock the mystery of adolescent metamorphosis. Gilbert acknowledges his own experiences as a professional educator and parent with insight and humility. His intelligent and comprehensive discussion can benefit both parents and professionals. Without being condescending or judgmental, he invites the reader to consider how to navigate this most poignant time in a child's life. His approach to the most daunting subjects is evenhanded and optimistic. The reader can easily access the information and leave feeling encouraged and hopeful. Dr. Gilbert masterfully reminds us all of the importance of being the caring adult to a child undergoing this amazing transformation. The joys and benefits of making this journey are well worth the 'roller-coaster ride.' This book should be required reading for every adult making the trip!"

—Janice Sjöstrand, educator, vocalist, and motivational speaker

"In experiencing the adolescence of my own son and daughter, I found relevance in Dr. Michael Gilbert's book from start to finish. As I teach and train in the field of leadership, I share that leaders do not need to have all the right answers yet must be comfortable embracing tough questions and circumstances. The same could be said for parents and caregivers of adolescents. This book makes that connection! Gilbert's chapters are straightforward, practical, and timely—thoughtfully written with respect to challenges of adolescent identity and what we can do to celebrate it. I recommend this book to all who appreciate helpful straight talk, delivered sensitively. A very good read!"

—Ryan Donlan, chair, Department of Teaching and Learning; associate professor, educational leadership, Indiana State University

Surviving Adolescence

Helping Teens Endure the Roller-Coaster Ride

MICHAEL B. GILBERT

ROWMAN & LITTLEFIELD
Lanham • Boulder • New York • London

Published by Rowman & Littlefield
A wholly owned subsidiary of The Rowman & Littlefield Publishing Group, Inc.
4501 Forbes Boulevard, Suite 200, Lanham, Maryland 20706
www.rowman.com

6 Tinworth Street, London, SE11 5AL, United Kingdom

British Library Cataloguing in Publication Information Available

Library of Congress Control Number: 2020950816

ISBN: 978-1-4758-5725-2 (cloth : alk. paper)
ISBN: 978-1-4758-5724-5 (electronic)

♾™ The paper used in this publication meets the minimum requirements of
American National Standard for Information Sciences—Permanence of Paper
for Printed Library Materials, ANSI/NISO Z39.48-1992.

Contents

Preface

This book was written because the most trying times in a child's life are during adolescence, and most parents and teachers may be ill-equipped to deal effectively with adolescents. The ideas have come from professional preparation and experience, and personal observation and trials in parenting.

My professional arena in schools, classrooms, and the world at large has given me opportunities to work with and observe youngsters. My home has provided the intimate site for practice. I also serve as a *Guardian ad Litem*, advocating for children who have been removed from their homes because of violence, neglect, or abuse.

I have not always been successful in parenting, but I think my batting average is respectable, judging by the accomplished and loving adults my children (all four) have become. I bring you ideas that are not mine alone. I have borrowed from others.

I do not come to you saying I have all of the answers. I am not even sure I know all of the questions. I hope my experiences and ideas will help you to be more successful in your parenting, classroom interactions, or other relationships you have with teens.

I tried to target parents and teachers who are about to begin the adolescent experience of their children and students. Those of you who are years from parenting adolescents or have blooming adolescents may find some useful tools on this roller-coaster ride filled with vacillating emotions and developing independence. For those of you whose children are parents or are about to become parents, maybe some of these ideas will be useful as you enter a new chapter with grandchildren, nieces, and nephews.

Teachers and school counselors may benefit from the ideas presented here. The conceptual and emotional changes adolescents experience can be amplified or abated depending on the sensitivity to their issues. Considerations should include the curriculum, instructional management, and teaching strategies.

The works of Herman Epstein, P. S. George, William Alexander, and John Santrock are worthy of note. They recognized that prepubescent and early adolescents, "tweenagers," are different from the children they were and the adolescents they are becoming.

In another vein, I wrestled with the issue of gender-specific pronouns. To eliminate some of the awkwardness of the he/she construction, I decided to alternate chapters. One chapter will be decidedly feminine in construction, while the next will be masculine.

I hope you will find the ideas not only humorous and familiar, but most of all, helpful and resourceful. Finally, I trust you will survive adolescence and find many more ways to love and respect your children, and assist them on their journey to healthy, happy independence and a more enjoyable life. May your roller-coaster rides be confined to theme parks.

RELATED READINGS

Epstein, H. T. (1990). Stages in human mental growth. *Journal of Educational Psychology, 82*(4): 876–80.

Faber, A., & Mazlish, E. (2005). *How to talk so teens will listen and listen so teens will talk.* New York: HarperCollins.

George, P. S., & Alexander, W. M. (1993). *The exemplary middle school* (2nd ed.). Orlando, FL: Holt, Rinehart and Winston.

KidsHealth. (2015). Talking with your child about puberty. *Kidshealth.org*. Available at: https://kidshealth.org/en/parents/talk-about-puberty.html, retrieved October 11, 2019.

Phelan T. W. (2012). *Surviving your adolescents: How to manage and let go of your 13–18 year olds* (3rd ed.). Glen Ellyn, IL: Parentmagic.

Phelan, T. W. (2016). *1-2-3 magic teen: Communicate, connect, and guide your teen to adulthood* (4th ed.). Naperville, IL: Sourcebooks.

Rice, F. P., & Dolgin, K. G. (2008). *The adolescent: Development, relationships, and culture* (12th ed.). Upper Saddle River, NJ: Pearson.

Rosemond, J. (1998). *Teen-proofing: Fostering responsible decision-making in your teenager*. Kansas City, MO: Andrews McMeel.

Santrock, J. W. (2019). *Adolescence* (17th ed.). New York: McGraw-Hill.

Siegel, D. J. (2014). *Brainstorm: The power and purpose of the teenage brain*. New York: TarcherPerigee.

Vann, M. R. (2009). Talking with your child about puberty. *Everyday Health, Inc.* Available at: https://www.everydayhealth.com/kids-health/talking -about-puberty.aspx, retrieved 11 October 2019.

Acknowledgments

I thank my children for the parenting lessons they taught me as they grew into adults. All four are different with wonderful talents and interesting perspectives.

My thanks to Dr. Ryan Donlan, associate professor of educational leadership at Indiana State University; Dr. Nanette Johnson Curiskis, professor emerita from Minnesota State University, Mankato; Dr. Angela Sewall, dean emerita of the College of Education at the University of Arkansas at Little Rock; and Dr. Mindy Kronenberg, a psychologist specializing in issues of children, for their review of my writing and their helpful suggestions.

I appreciate the works of Dr. William Alexander, the father of the middle school, and Dr. John Santrock, for his work on adolescence.

Finally, I admire adolescents—past, current, and future—for negotiating what might be the hardest part of their lives. Coping with their miraculous physical, emotional, social, and hormonal changes deserves kudos.

Part I

RATCHETING UP

1

Preparation for Adolescence/Adolescents

Adolescence is a time when optimal development is stimulated through exploration, making and learning from mistakes, and trying on identities. (National Education Policy Center, 2019)

WHAT IS AN ADOLESCENT?

An adolescent is:

a weight watcher who goes on a diet by giving up candy bars before breakfast

a youngster who receives her allowance on Monday, spends it on Tuesday, and borrows from her best friend on Wednesday

someone who can hear a (popular) song three blocks away but not his mother calling from the next room

a whiz who can operate the latest electronic device without a lesson but can't make a bed

a student who will spend twelve minutes studying for her history exam and twelve hours studying for her driver's license an enthusiast who has the energy to ride a bike for miles but is usually too tired to dry the dishes

a connoisseur of two kinds of music—loud and very loud

a young woman who loves the cat and tolerates her brother

a person who is always late for dinner but always on time for a (pop music) concert

a romantic who never falls in love more than once a week

a budding beauty who never smiles until her braces come off

a boy who can sleep until noon on any Saturday when he suspects the lawn needs mowing

an original thinker who is positive that her mother never was a teenager. (Adler, 1986)

Youngsters between the ages of 10 and 14 are a unique and special group of people. They are no longer children who are wholly dependent on their parents and other adults for guidance and direction, but neither are they totally self-sufficient.

These preadolescents and early adolescents—"tweenagers"—are mystified by the changes they are experiencing. They are going through the most remarkable and scary time of their lives as they enter puberty and emerge as *adolescents.*

Most adults who live and work with these special people are not prepared for the remarkable changes that occur. The most noticeable change is *physical.* The long bones begin their final massive growth—pants seem to get shorter day by day; full-length skirts become miniskirts in what seems like only a week or two. Hips get wider, and chests get broader. Struggling children get much stronger, and voices get deeper. Whiskers appear. And there is the exciting/traumatic shopping trip for the first bra.

Puberty takes about a year and a half to three years to complete. Youngsters have difficulty during this period. Some have been known to trip on lint in the carpet. Others have been heard to sing soprano one day and squeaky baritone the next. Still others can begin to solve higher-order mathematical problems, yet have trouble following simple directions for setting the dinner table.

In addition to the physical growth surge, adolescents also grow *emotionally, socially,* and *intellectually,* and in their *ability to coordinate* their bodies. They have an increased need for "fuel," which is why they seem to be eating constantly.

Their body regulators are shifting. They may have boundless energy at some times and are listless at other times. They also are more able to deal with abstractions but are confused by romantic feelings.

One of the most profound changes is in their need for identity and independence. The roller-coaster ride has begun.

They are confronted with the question of self-concept: Who am I? What am I? Why am I here? What am I capable of doing? Parents and teachers are observing an individual going through the remarkable changes—the *metamorphosis*—called puberty.

Suddenly, the baby that you have loved and cared for seems to have turned into an egocentric chameleon. Where is your lovable child, and will she ever return? What happened to that sweet and compliant elementary school child?

CONFUSION

Many parents feel confused when their children enter their adolescent years. Nothing they have experienced up to this point in their lives has prepared them for the emotional roller-coaster ride that confronts them.

Do the children survive? Probably. Do the parents survive? Most likely. This time in the relationship of parent and child will be a time of more in-depth power struggles and testing of boundaries.

PREPARATION

How do you prepare yourself for children's adolescence? Preparation should begin at a much earlier time in the child's life than at the brink of adolescence.

When the child is still a small being and the parent plays a much larger role in helping form an impression, the child can and should be given unconditional love, self-worth, encouragement, and increasing independence.

Independence is not total freedom of behavior and lack of structure, but rather a gradual progression into appropriate decision making. The youngster makes decisions that are appropriately hers and accepts the consequences of those decisions.

> Our society does a poor job of making a place for adolescents. (Societal) changes . . . have left adolescents in a social and psychological no-man's land. They can consume, but not produce; they can be educated, but not apply the education; they have increasing independence, but often no greater responsibilities than getting their homework done and keeping their rooms clean. Rapid technology has created a knowledge gap between generations; divorce and separation leave many adolescents isolated from adults who can serve as role models (Taibbi, 1990, p. 33).

When adults become parents, the resource they have to draw upon is how they were parented. In many respects, people are as good at parenting as what their parents were. They can choose to improve on what they experienced for the benefit of their own children, as well as for their own growth. (Teachers also fall prey to repeating the pattern of their own history. They tend to teach as they were taught.)

How can there be improvement in your own parenting compared to how you were parented? Look back at your own childhood and remember the things you wished had been different. You may have wanted your parents to have listened to you more, given you more freedom of choice, offered their respect, or given you a hug of assurance when you were afraid or apprehensive about something.

You may have said you would never do what your parents did to you. When your children frustrate you, it is amazing how much of what you say echoes those things you said you would never say or do. Hmm!

The change can be anything you felt was missing in your childhood. The gaps can be filled by whatever you may choose to add to your own child's life.

I experienced a change in my own parenting one day when my son spilled his milk. He is extraordinarily coordinated, so being clumsy was not something I expected in him. (He was about 10 or 11 at the time.)

My initial response would have been to be critical and berate him. (That was what I experienced from my father.) But I stopped, took a breath, and finally said, "You better get something quickly to wipe up the milk."

He looked at me to be sure he recognized the person who was talking, then he got some paper towels. He was still a bit surprised and confused.

I realized that I had been treating one of the dearest people in my life somewhat abusively. I would never fuss at a guest who spilled his wine. I would respond with, "That's okay. We have more, and the wine will come out in the wash."

Why would I respond to a guest more politely?

CHANGING

How do you change? First, recognize the need: If what you're doing isn't working, stop. Find something that does work.

Repeating yourself will probably not work, even if you are louder. Instant replay, even from different angles, does not change history.

Next, look for resources to address whatever you see the problem to be. These may be as simple as talking to another parent whose opinion you respect. Or you may decide to find an expert—online or elsewhere. Or you may look for counseling from a trained professional.

When you find a suggestion or technique that seems to apply, try it. If you seem to accomplish what you want, if you see yourself as success-ful, evaluate the result and celebrate it.

If you have changed your behavior and your parenting is smoother (for the moment), keep doing whatever works until it doesn't. Then start over.

UNCONDITIONAL LOVE

The most important thing you can give to your child is *you*. If you start from that point of giving, the rest will evolve, and the rewards will be great.

Giving of yourself is the first step of unconditional love that every child needs and every child deserves. Unconditional love helps provide the basic foundation of the child's personality and self-esteem.

In the years to come this foundation will be a cushion against some of life's less pleasant experiences. You are building a relationship, the rewards of which will continue to accrue.

Unconditional love sounds easier than it really is, especially if it was not given to you. What may have to happen is that you first learn how to give unconditional love to yourself. Accept yourself in whatever you think and feel, and do not let the thoughts and feelings of childhood block your way in developing into whatever person you have chosen to be. You may not be the person your parents wanted you to be.

Recognize that thought or feeling for what it really is, your parents' issue. It is also a projection of what your parents probably wanted for themselves but were afraid to try because of their own upbringing. With unconditional love, you can be whatever it is you want to be and completely safe and sure you will be loved by those who are close to you.

Because most of the feelings we deal with in the family diverge from the predictable cycle of feelings handed down from parent to child, dealing with these old feelings usually takes place in our own adulthood and sometimes even after our parents are gone. Once we recognize this, we can give our children a great gift by breaking that cycle and beginning to deal with our own feelings from the past. Only then can we develop our own self-worth, as well as plant the seeds of self-worth in our own children.

With unconditional love as the strong foundation for children, the next important component in their development is self-worth. In giving the child firm footing to grow, we must not be impatient. Waiting is hard.

I remembered one morning when I discovered a cocoon in the bark of a tree, just as a butterfly was making a hole in its case and preparing to come out. I waited a while, but it was too long appearing and I was impatient. I bent over it and breathed on it to warm it. I warmed it as quickly as I could, and the miracle began to happen before my eyes, faster than life.

The case opened, the butterfly started slowly crawling out and I shall never forget my horror when I saw how its wings were folded back and crumpled; the wretched butterfly tried with its whole trembling body to unfold them. Bending over it, I tried to help it with my breath. In vain.

It needed to be hatched out patiently and the unfolding of the wings should be a gradual process in the sun. Now it was too late. My breath had forced the butterfly to appear, all crumpled, before its time. It struggled desperately and, a few seconds later, died in the palm of my hand.

> That little body is, I do believe, the greatest weight I have on my conscience. For I realize today that it is a mortal sin to violate the great laws of nature. We should not hurry, we should not be impatient, but we should confidently obey the eternal rhythm.— Kazantzakis, *Zorba the Greek*

Be patient. The butterfly in your child will emerge eventually, given loving support.

EDUCATIONAL CONSIDERATIONS

The changes the child experiences carry over into the classroom. School organizations recognized the developing individual and moved toward the middle school concept in the late 1960s. The grouping of burgeoning adolescents into a distinct and dedicated setting made sense.

Coupled with staffing the school with teachers who are trained to deal with adolescents and have enormous empathy for what their students are experiencing was a breakthrough. It is no longer appropriate simply to hire secondary teachers and place them in the middle school as content specialists only. The kids are special and require teachers who are prepared specially. Empathy is high on the list of required skills.

Survival Tips
- Adolescence happens; it is the difficult but exciting path to adulthood.
- Most parents and teachers are not ready.
- Take care of yourself first; you need to be energized.
- Love the child unconditionally.
- Be patient.
- Respect the change.

REFERENCES

Adler, B. (1986). *What is a teenager?* New York: Bill Adler Books.

National Education Policy Center (NEPC). (2019, August 8). Adolescence: Six facts to know. *NEPC Newsletter*, p. 1. Available at: https://nepc.colorado. edu/publication/newsletter-adolescence-080819, retrieved 9 January 2020.

Taibbi, R. (1990, July/August). The uninitiated. *Family Therapy Networker*, pp. 30–35.

2

What Have You Done with My Child?

WHEN PREADOLESCENCE HITS

Preadolescence can begin anytime from ages 10 to 14 years. Each child's experience with preadolescence will be different and unique.

This time of change can be relatively smooth and bump-free to the beginning of a raging storm or the wildest roller coaster in the park. You might wonder what all the fuss is about preadolescent behavior, or you might be wondering where your sweet child has gone and who left this monster in its place.

Your mantra should be: "This is the normal process to adulthood." Your child has now begun the arduous journey to adulthood by beginning to break away from the safety and security of your protection.

You are no longer seen as perfect—in fact, you are quite the opposite. You are suspect about almost everything you say and do. You will get more, "Why do I have to do that?" Compliance wanes, and defiance emerges.

You begin to feel yourself falling from the wonderful heights of that pedestal of your child's admiration. Say this: "This is the normal process to adulthood." No, really. Don't just read it. Say it!

Hold on tight!

Be firm!

Be flexible!
Offer guidance!
Listen (more about this later)!
Back off (within a safe distance)!
Keep strong (but reasonable) boundaries!
Admit your mistakes!
Enjoy your budding adolescent!
Most of all, know things will calm down with time.

REMEMBER THE ALAMO
No, this is not a lesson about Texas history, but guidance to remember your own adolescent experience. It was your history. Remembering what happened to you will help you understand what your child might be experiencing. Issues and challenges that confront your children may be different from yours, but the basics of adolescence are still there.

You are a generation away. What confronts your child now may have little resemblance to what the world was like when you were entering your teens.

Recalling what it felt like to have those fears, those impulses, those pressures, those attractions and how you dealt with them can help in easing the difficulties your child is having. You may have been confused by wanting your space but also wanting the protection of a nearby parent.

You wanted answers to yet unspoken questions. Mostly, you wanted to know what was going on and what would happen next.

Since you are at this point in your life, you obviously survived your own adolescence. What helped you negotiate the bumps and turns?

Be strong and hold on for the roller-coaster ride. Know your sweet child will return as a grown person: "This is the normal process to adulthood."

KEEPING YOUR SENSE OF HUMOR
Some of the things that can happen and some of the things your adolescent might say can be quite bizarre. Do not to take everything your adolescent says too seriously. But don't ignore serious issues.

Your decisions about what goes on in the life of your child will be questioned more. "Why?" becomes more frequent.

Adolescents will ask why until they understand. Even then, they may nettle you if they don't agree with your answer. They will try to be in greater control of the decisions they think affect them.

"Because I said so" is no longer an acceptable answer. The youngster wants to understand the rationale or justification. Be prepared to explain!

Be on the lookout for abnormal behavior, especially with regard to body image and peer pressure. Anorexia and bulimia can hit teeange girls the hardest. Boys worry about whether they can measure up to the other guys—the *top dogs*.

Be careful to laugh *with* them, not *at* them. Their egos are very fragile, regardless of the *front* they offer.

Sometimes, they do funny or ridiculous things. We cannot help laughing, but we say, "I am not laughing *at* you; I'm just laughing *near* you." (Be careful of being dismissive or sarcastic.) Teasing is not something teens (and others) respond to positively.

Mom asked her child to put on his shoes. He did so awkwardly and incorrectly. She said, "Those are the wrong feet."
Without hesitation he replied, "No. I am sure these are my feet."
What's right is what's left after everything else is wrong.

Many adolescents will practice their *attitudes* with others. They have a different way of responding to their peers and others than what they reserve for parents and other adults. The loudest salvos are reserved for those closest to them.

We can either be tolerant of or ignore inappropriate behaviors and remarks, or we can correct their words and tones. We are asking them to change. Trying to force them to change is most futile and frustrating when they do not comply (cf. Tobias, 2012).

Try to motivate them to be respectful with their words and deeds, but also give them some space for individual personality quirks. You must figure out which is happening at any given time and act appropriately.

> There once was a little boy who had a bad temper. His father gave him a bag of nails and told him every time he lost his temper, he must hammer a nail into the back of the fence. The first day, the boy had driven thirty-seven nails into the fence. During the next few weeks, as he learned to control his anger, the number of nails hammered daily gradually dwindled down. He discovered it was easier to hold his temper than to drive those nails into the fence.
>
> Finally, the day came when the boy didn't lose his temper at all. He told his father about it, and the father suggested the boy now pull out one nail for each day he was able to hold his temper. The days passed, and the boy was finally able to tell his father all the nails were gone. The father took his son by the hand and led him to the fence. He said, "You have done well, my son, but look at the holes in the fence. The fence will never be the same. When you say things in anger, they leave a scar just like this one. You can put a knife in a man and draw it out. It won't matter how many times you say I'm sorry, the wound is still there. A verbal wound is as bad as a physical one."

In trying to find their place in the world, adolescents may not consider how their words and actions affect others. They can be mean to others. (See more in chapter 10, "Bullying.") Trying to put the toothpaste back in the tube doesn't work. One of the important lessons is teaching adolescents to think before they speak; teasing others cannot be undone. Saying "I'm sorry" doesn't remove the hurt.

This is just one of life's lesson to teach. It can be a battle. You have to ask yourself if this is a battle worth waging? Sometimes it is better to choose what you battle about, so you can ultimately win the "war."

The challenge is there are no rules to help you decide. Whether you stand your ground or give way depends on your mood, attitude, and emotional (and physical) energy. (It is crucial you get your own needs met *regularly* to have the required energy and stamina to deal with your changing child.)

DECISION-MAKING BASICS

Adolescents need to find themselves and discover their own personal style and space. What better way to give them the space to discover by supporting their desire to dress as they wish and decorate their rooms in a way that appeals to them. Again, keep your sense of humor, but set your limits on what is allowed.

Yes, bizarre hair color may abound in public, but they do not need to mimic everything they see. Yes, it is their bedroom, but they do not get to knock out a wall to make it more appealing.

Discuss with your adolescent what the boundaries are, and let him know what will be his responsibilities in the upkeep (if any) with his new self and abode. When he hears he will need to pitch in, be prepared for weeping, wailing, snarling, and sniping. Be prepared for intense negotiations, or maybe even the silent treatment.

Whatever tactic your teen decides to take, set limits, hold fast to what is not negotiable (this is tricky!), and make him accountable. (More on this later.)

If he participates more in the decision making that affects him, he may ultimately agree to a fair outcome. Occasionally, you may have to make a decision without agreement and without further argument. (Some things are not negotiable. You'll figure out what they are.)

There may be a delicate balance between what is negotiable and what is not. Be sure whatever pattern you set, you stay consistent. If you say, "It's your decision," you will have to support what he decides. If you are not willing to support decisions without boundaries, then participate with him in making a decision, keeping veto power to use, if necessary.

It is up to you to set the stage for future control issues to come. One thing must be honored: Once a decision has been made and agreed upon, stick with the decision (unless conditions change).

If you invite him to participate, he has some ownership of the decision. Sometimes, it will be a shared decision. Sometimes, it will be his alone. Sometimes, it will be only yours.

Regardless of whether you share in the decision making, exerting your parental authority in *his* decisions will only create resentment and mistrust: "Well, you said I could decorate my room."

Revoking his right to decide after it has been given to him means you may have not examined the situation closely enough or not set reasonable boundaries. He will be suspicious the next time you say, "It's your decision."

He can see only the small picture—his body and his room. You are responsible for his safety and the home he lives in with you.

You are now setting the norm—the pattern—for all future power struggles or negotiations. You are his peripheral vision and moral compass.

At some point, you must back off and let him live with the consequences of his decisions. This is hard, but it is the beginning of their true independence. If you give it to him and then take it away, be prepared to face many more struggles down the road or accept the damage, tranistory as it may be, to your credibility in his eyes.

Maturing is interesting. We rush through our early lives, wanting to hurry the growth process. At some point, we look back and want to recapture some of what we have lost.

An older man encountered a youngster sitting on the curb crying. He asked what was wrong. The little fellow said, "I can't do what the big boys do." The older man sat down and cried with him.

EDUCATIONAL CONSIDERATIONS

In the early part of the twentieth century, the junior high school emerged. It was a way of relieving some of the overcrowding at the high school because of a growing propulation. It was, indeed, *junior*, mostly because of the ages and sizes of the students. The curriculum was organized similarly to the high school.

Many districts adopted the grade organization of seventh and eighth or seventh through ninth grades for the junior high school and ninth through twelfth or tenth through twelfth grades for the (senior) high school. That school organization still exists today in many school districts.

Today, we may see both a junior high school and a middle (or intermediate) school between the elementary school and the high school. The grade organizations vary.

The justification for the middle school was the identification that youngsters ages 10 through 14 were no longer children but not yet full-fledged teenagers. They needed something other than the sheltered environment of most elementary schools and a transition into the departmentalization of the high school.

One thought was to have a mostly self-contained environment during the first year (usually grade 6), moving into a balance of self-containment and departmentalization during the second year, and mostly departmentalization during the third year. Additionally, attention was paid to the social and emotional needs of the changing student (cf. George & Alexander, 1993).

While many of the changes are remarkable and visible during early adolescence, conceptual ability also changes dramatically, as the brain matures. Student ability to move from the concrete to the abstract becomes more widespread with each year (cf. Epstein, 1981, 1990; Epstein & Toepfer, 1978).

Moving too quickly into abstract concepts (for example, algebra) can confound the immature brain and frustrate the student. When exposed to the yet unknown quantity of x, the student wants to know what x is. He is told it is unknown. Huh?

Survival Tips

- Hold on tight! It may be a bumpy ride.
- Developing competent decision makers is an important part of developing independence in adolescents.
- Winning the battle may not win the war.
- Avoid as many battles as you can.
- Recognize all of the dramatic changes in the youngster—social, emotional, physical, and conceptual.

REFERENCES

Epstein, H. T. (1981, May). Learning to learn: Matching instruction to cognitive levels. *Principal, 60*(5): 25–30. (ERIC Document Accession No. EJ248432)

Fpstein, H. T. (1990). Stages in human mental growth. *Journal of Educational Psychology, 82*(4): 876–80.

Epstein, H. T., & Toepfer, C. F., Jr. (1978, May). A neuroscience basis for reorganizing middle grades education. *Educational Leadership, 35*(8): 656–58, 660. (ERIC Document Accession No. EJ179251)

George, P. S., & Alexander, W. M. (1993). *The exemplary middle school* (2nd ed.). Orlando, FL: Holt, Rinehart and Winston.

Tobias, C. U. (2012). *You can't make me (but I can be persuaded): Strategies for bringing out the best in your strong-willed child* (Rev. ed.). Colorado Springs, CO: WaterBrook Press.

3

Strong Partners, Effective Parenting

United We Stand—Divided We Fall . . . Flat on Our Faces

(The historical pattern has been that parents will be married to one another. Today's family units see adults in other types of relationships.)

Being in a strong relationship is crucial for parents when their children's adolescence approaches. The challenges magnify.

For adults to be effective in their roles as parents, a partnership is imperative. At times, battle lines will seem to have been drawn. If the children know their parents do not have a united front, those same sweet children will do everything they can to break those lines and try to win their position. The point here is not have lines drawn at all, with no (or few) battles.

Foremost, the partner parents work as teams. They should discuss expectations and procedures for dealing with the children. Each should consult the other on important issues—to agree or to discuss the most appropriate way to deal with their children.

PARENTING UNITS

The makeup of parent configurations has changed so much in the last few decades. Today, a family unit can be made up of a mother and father married to one another, as well as a cornucopia of variations.

No matter what parental unit there is, everyone needs to have strong relationships within that unit, and strong support systems outside of the parental unit as well. One configuration is not necessarily better than another.

If you are reading this book, you are interested in being the best parent you can be and raising well-adjusted children into well-adjusted adults. It does not matter if you are in a traditional two-parent relationship or a single parent or in a two-partner relationship, or any other possibility.

The point is we all want to do what is best for our children. We all may experience the same pain, anger, doubt, and frustration when it comes to parenting.

Tradition

The birth-mother and birth-father families are not gone, but they may be fewer. This configuration would describe the mother as the primary nurturer and caregiver to the children, and the keeper of the home, while the father is the major breadwinner and provider of lawn care and automotive maintenance. Today, the roles can be reversed—the father may be the primary nurturer and caregiver of children, while the mother is the major income provider.

What is far more likely and realistic in today's economy is that both parents work outside the home and inside the home with varying degrees of division of parental and household responsibilities. No matter what the role is, one necessary component is to have a strong, supportive, and stable relationship that will provide the children with a firm foundation for growth.

For parents to be effective, they must have a strong marriage. Both parents are united in a strong relationship.

Here the analogy of an oxygen mask may work. On airline flights, if the cabin pressure drops, passengers are told to put on their own mask first, then assist others. The same goes for marriages. If you don't take

STRONG PARTNERS, EFFECTIVE PARENTING

care of yourself first, your ability to help others may diminish and vanish if you pass out.

How can a couple build a strong relationship to withstand the stress and strain of parenthood? They must know one another very well, have good communication skills, be good friends, have a great sense of humor, participate in periodic date nights without the children, know when to listen and when to talk (see Faber & Mazlish, 2005), be quick with a hug and slow with a harsh word—the list can go on and on. The point is to have a strong and healthy relationship.

For the marriage to be top priority means, among other things, that the couple function primarily in the roles of partners (Rosemond, 2006). This many seem an unorthodox way to begin parenting, but marriage is the usual progression of the couple's relationship.

It is only fitting that this primary relationship stay primary, with the roles of parents taking a secondary position to the more important roles of loving partners. It is the strong foundation of the family to raise your children into healthy, happy, and well-adjusted adults.

No one starts out saying something such as, "I'd like to raise some really self-absorbed, insecure kids." If your focus becomes more toward a child-oriented household, you will end up with self-absorbed, insecure adults.

Why? Because you haven't taught them the world wasn't made for them without consideration of others, and you haven't given them the skills to adapt to life outside their "perfect" world. If you are successful in preparing your children for independence, will you have anything to help you reattach yourself to the person you married all those years ago after the children are gone, or will you both be strangers wondering what to do next? Think of your children as the icing on the cake, with you and your spouse as the cake.

When the spouses are called to parenting duty, the parents *partner* as one unit. They should discuss expectations and procedures for dealing with the children. Each should consult the other on issues of importance—to get concurrence or discuss what seems to be the most appropriate way of dealing with a given situation.

All strategies and plans of action should be discussed in private. Throughout time, the parental partners will work as a well-oiled machine, and they can both act as two even when one is not present—keep the major issues to be discussed for when both parents are together.

Parental partners should agree with one another as much as possible. Disagreeing respectfully when it comes to issues involving the children is okay, especially if the children are contributing to the decision.

> I've learned that if you want to do something positive for your children, try to improve your marriage. (Anonymous, age 61)

Single Parenting

Single parenting in and of itself can be tremendously draining, because you are called upon to be both mother and father to your children. As with a couple, you must keep yourself the foundation of the household.

Even though you are called upon to be everything to everyone, it is imperative you keep yourself healthy, focused, and energized. If there is another parent but not in the home, this can alleviate some of the overwhelming responsibilities of child rearing. For many the reality is that she or he is the lone parent.

How can you help yourself? Seek out support systems within your community to help with the overwhelming responsibilities that come with single parenthood. Many associations and support groups can help with services you may need (Parents without Partners, etc.). Local religious organizations can offer a spiritual outlet to meet other social needs that you or your children may have.

A person does not have to experience parenthood alone unless that is the road the parent chooses. The most important thing is to keep yourself energized, so you can endure the various issues you will be called upon to face as a parent.

Divorced Parenting

In a perfect world, people fall in love, marry, have children, and raise their little ones to adulthood together. But the world is not perfect. People fall out of love, get bored, find their needs met elsewhere, change, decide they do not want to be married anymore, and a long list of other variations. For whatever the reason, half of marriages in the United States end in divorce (data from 2018).

Divorce happens, and often the children are left confused, angry, sad, possibly blaming themselves—wondering what will happen to them. Divorce has a huge impact on children, even if they are better off with their parents' separation.

If the child is also dealing with adolescence, the confusion can be overwhelming. Just as with parents who stay together, the custodial parent must provide a strong foundation for her or his children, so they can adjust to the loss and their new living arrangement.

Stepparenting

People who marry someone who already has children or bring children into a marriage have special challenges. The guidance of being a parental unit still applies. It will not work if the stepparent defers or disengages, saying, "Well, she's your child. You deal with her."

If the stepparent has not already been a parent, the learning curve is steep. In addition to establishing a respectful, loving relationship with the child, the techniques of parenting have to be effective as quickly as possible. This must happen regardless of whether the child lives with you full-time or not.

The vestige of the absent parent may loom. If your style is different from your predecessor's, you may hear, "That's not how Mom does it" or "I wish my dad was here."

This can sting. What must be clear are the rules in your home (decided by both parent partners). These are what the child must respect. (Of course, it is better if the rules in both homes are similar.)

Be careful of criticizing your parent counterpart's behavior. Discuss any major difference of expectations and boundaries between the adults of both homes.

PARENTING TAKES WORK

Regardless of the composition of the parenting unit, accept that you must work hard to guide your child effectively. You are always *on call*. Remember to take care of yourself first. Do not be so selfless as to put the children first without sufficient emotional energy.

Know what you need and find consistent ways to fill those needs. Take time for yourself to be a better parent.

EDUCATIONAL CONSIDERATIONS

Providing guidance for the adolescent also involves teachers. It is important the school staff also partner with the parents. Periodic communication between the school and home serves to support the growing and changing adolescent.

What happens at home can be transmitted to the classroom environment. Collaterally, what happens at school can be carried home.

Starting the day well with a good breakfast (stoking the teenage metabolic furnace) can lead to a positive start at school. Similarly, a good day at school can begin with positive family time at home. (Breakfast programs at school should be available to all students.)

If the teachers are prepared to interact positively with the youngsters, any problems that arise can be addressed at the moment. Ignoring hints and symptoms can lead to possibly explosive situations, which may or may not follow the smaller issues.

We have to be watchful of what is going on. Do not presume that no "noise" means there are not problems.

Survival Tips

- Coordinate boundaries and expectations with your parent partner.
- Involve your adolescent in decisions.
- Keep an absent parent engaged.
- Meet your own needs.
- Stay in touch with others who interact with your adolescent regularly.
- Keep your partnerships strong.

REFERENCES

Faber, A., & Mazlish, E. (2005). *How to talk so teens will listen and listen so teens will talk*. New York: HarperCollins.

Rosemond, J. (2006). *The new six-point plan for raising happy, healthy children*. Kansas City, MO: Andrews McMeel.

4

The Family as a Unit

RESPONSIBILITIES

Each member of a family has certain responsibilities, certain obligations that go along with family membership. Adolescents, who are fast approaching adulthood, have rights and responsibilities, as well.

Children's rights are to be treated with appropriate respect and cared for in safe environments. Parents need to provide adequate food and clothing, as a minimum.

Responsibilities of each family member are determined jointly. A good way to start is to have periodic family meetings, usually when there is not a pressing issue or crisis. Focus on the needs of each family member. (Stating what one needs is a key component of assertiveness, and assertiveness is an important skill for self-assured adults.)

One of the most important aspects of family living is *interdependence*—family members depend on one another. Their lives are dramatically intertwined.

Parents have the responsibilities of providing shelter, food, clothing, and a nurturing and loving environment in which children can develop into healthy individuals. Children should not be the unhappy result of hormones gone wild.

Author's note: I have often advocated, without hope of bringing the idea into reality, that parents should be licensed. If people want to have children, they should have to pass a licensing examination and a practical test before conception occurs, so there is some certainty that children will be raised by responsible and capable parents.

Of course, this is not realistic, but it is an interesting notion. If we insist people know the "Rules of the Road" and have to pass a performance test before a driver's license is issued, how can we look at parenthood less seriously?!

The outcomes of poor parenting have much greater and longer-lasting consequences than most instances of poor driving. The need for *Guardians ad Litem* for the local legal system has demonstrated the dire effects of poor parenting. These individuals, usually volunteers, represent the interests of the children in situations where the children have been removed from the home because of abuse, neglect, or violence.

Children have responsibilities as members of the family, as well. Their resources are limited, but they should be expected to contribute what they can. Some of the things with which they can assist are keeping the common living areas clean and pleasant, respecting the rights and space of others, being an active member of the family, sharing in family decisions, and providing love and role-appropriate emotional support for parents. (Yes, adults need affection, too. They need *oxygen* to function skillfully and properly.)

ALLOWANCE
The issue of when and whether a child is given spending money is an important one. This may be the first instance of freedom from parental control and responsibility for one's actions. When a youngster can

count and know the value of coins and paper money may be the time when getting an allowance begins. The amount is not as important as learning the responsibility each child has in the family. A reasonable guideline is to start with some pocket change for preschoolers, advancing to $1 for each year of age once a child gets into school. Of course, family income and number of children may also be used to decide allowance amounts. (In some cases, adolescents work outside the home to contribute to family income.)

Children should be guided to keep the amount of money they have confidential. They should not advertise what they have. Others, especially with teens, may seek to take advantage.

Getting an allowance is a means of determining buying decisions without close parental supervision. It may allow a youngster to buy something special for himself. Parents may need to provide guidelines for appropriate uses of money. For example, if candy is not permissible, youngsters need to know that ahead of time.

This can also begin the time when the parent teaches the youngster about saving money to accumulate enough to buy more expensive items or spend the money on others. It is important to stress that control of the actual money is the youngster's.

If he chooses to spend it on something totally frivolous, that is all right. If that whim means he is without money for something else, the consequence is clear. There is only so much that he has to spend—when it is gone, it is gone.

Parents should be careful of rescuing their children from poor decisions. The message of "If I screw up, mom or dad will save me" can be disabling and dangerous. If children feel entitled to anything and everything, they may become self-centered and selfish.

At the same time the youngster is given an allowance, he may also be given household responsibilities to share—emptying the trash, dusting the furniture, clearing the table, etc. When a parent begins to expect a youngster to share in the responsibilities of the home, it is important he is taught how to do each activity. The parent should spend a sufficient amount of time teaching the child the steps of each task and then observe the child as he performs that task at the outset.

Each task should be done periodically and usually as often as is necessary. Sometimes, when the child returns from school is an appropriate time to do those things that are not meal-centered. "Before you start your homework, be sure your chores are done."

Rotating chores monthly (if there is more than one child in the home) is helpful. Post a list of who is to do what. (*Parents* should be on the list, as well. It is important parents participate in household responsibilities in the same way that they expect the children to perform their responsibilities.)

Because taking care of a home is a *chore*, not everyone will take on the task eagerly. In fact, procrastination is seen often with some of the tasks. Are there things to keep the house clean and in order postponed until company is expected? When those tasks are performed, it is not unlikely to hear, "Who's coming to visit?"

It is important that you let your children know that you, as a family, are as important as your guests. When the living space is clean and orderly, it is because you all deserve to live in a nice home and you can be proud of where you live.

Chores may intrude on other more pleasant things. It is more fun to watch TV, listen to music, or play video games than to vacuum the floors. It is important you stress the responsibilities each youngster has. It is necessary they be done in a consistent fashion.

When a youngster fails to perform his household responsibilities, there are consequences. Nominal *deductions* from allowance, communicated in advance, are appropriate. Conversely, if the youngster takes on more than his fair share of what is expected, it is reasonable for him to expect to receive *credit* for additional responsibilities. This credit may be in cash or additional privileges or acknowledgment. (Some are motivated by tangible rewards. Others may prefer something that affirms who they are—a hug, a "gold star" to put on the door to their room, etc.)

Allowance is given as spending money for being a family member. A parent should be careful not to make it seem as if the child is an employee of a household corporation. He should feel proud to be a member of the family and that it is appropriate for him to share in the activities of the home. Having his own spending money helps him to develop decisions and values with respect to being a responsible consumer.

[Note: While responsibility may be an important personal and family value, it may not be embraced by all children, especially if they are oriented to external motivation, like play.]

LOVING YOUR CHILDREN

Most children are conceived in love and are an expression of the deep caring and attachment parents have for one another. Children need love to thrive and survive.

Parents sometimes withhold love or forget their child's need for love. Adolescents, in particular, need to be told or shown they are loved. They may be difficult to love at times.

Part of adolescence is testing the boundaries of their lives: "How far can I go and still have people love me?" Your love for your child must be unconditional, but you do not always have to like what he does.

The distinction needs to be clear. "I may not like what you do from time to time, but I will always love you."

When your child acts inappropriately, he needs to be told or reminded some behavior is inappropriate and will not be tolerated. There are consequences he must accept. Not fulfilling one's household responsibilities may mean that until the tasks are completed, the youngster may not go out, watch television, use electronic devices, etc.

It is important we treat our children as valued people. Many times, we treat the guests in our home better than we treat our own offspring. We may show greater respect for those who enter our lives casually than we do for the children who are very much a part of us.

If a guest spills red wine on a beautiful lace tablecloth, we shudder and wonder if there will be a stain. We scurry to wipe up the spill and reassure the guest that everything is all right.

If a child causes the same spill, we do not mask our dismay and anger. We may yell about how clumsy the youngster is and how he never listens when we tell him about paying attention to what he is doing.

We would probably never yell at a guest or ask him to leave the table. Why then should we treat our child any less respectfully?

What is important is that the spill be cleaned. It, of course, cannot be undone.

The child can be instructed to clean up, and we may want to help. The child is probably sorry for his lack of attention or clumsiness, without being embarrassed further.

Acknowledge the incident is unfortunate, but accidents do happen. You might go so far as to remind him that the glass could be moved farther back onto the table, out of harm's way.

The point is that we show the child that we love him and will continue to love him even when he is not doing things of which we are proud. But *withholding love as punishment* for inappropriate behavior can be highly damaging to the parent–adolescent relationship. The message the child receives is, "My parent will only love me if I behave well."

It is important that the youngster understands what is expected of him and that there are consequences for his decisions or actions. But he must also understand we will help when we can.

The key is he understands the difference between help and rescuing. You can assist with decisions by helping him to outline alternatives from which to choose, without making the choice for the youngster.

BLENDED FAMILIES

Widespread examples of marital discontent abound. People divorce in greater numbers or choose not to marry (U.S. Census Bureau, 2018). Divorce often involves more than just marital partners.

In most instances, children are caught up in the turmoil. Because divorce is seen more and more as a viable option, children of divorced partners may be very young. Decisions relating to where the children of divorced partners will live are varied, much more so than in the past. While the mother has been the typical custodial parent, now we see joint custody or custody with the father.

Regardless of where the children reside, there is still the huge emotional upset children undergo when they see their parents apart. Questions of guilt arise: "Was it my fault mommy and daddy got divorced?" "If I behave better, will mommy and daddy get back together?" Children are in great need of reassurance they are still loved and are not to blame.

Most people who marry once are likely to marry again. Custodial parents may be quicker to remarry because of a need to have a partner to share the responsibilities of caring for the children.

One major problem in remarriage, where blended (or reconstituted) families are created, is there may be some animosity or jealousy toward the new family members. The spouses want and need adult companionship and may resent the intrusion of stepchildren.

The "new" parent may be viewed suspiciously by the children or hated because that person has taken the place of the absent parent. At some point early in the relationship between the new parent and the children, there may be an expression of comparison or rejection: "My daddy used to do this" or "I wish my mommy was here."

Coming into a disjointed family can be just as difficult for the new parent as well. There are the *ghosts* of the previous marriage to battle and the establishment of a new set of expectations and behaviors.

What is important is both partners work on the expectations together and provide a united voice in dealing with the children. Expecting the children to check with both parents on important issues is highly reasonable, especially where the entire household might be affected.

Such may be the case when friends of the children may be invited to a meal or to be overnight guests. It is all right for one parent to say, "That's fine with me," as long as it is followed up with, "You also need to check with (the other parent) . . ."

What the new parent is called by the children needs to be decided as soon as a decision has been made to blend the family. Whatever the new parent is called should be something comfortable and respectful for everyone concerned.

First names are appropriate, as are "Mom" or "Dad." Children should not be forced to call the new parent something that might displace the absent parent. This may only cause additional strife.

Coming into a family with adolescents may be one of the most harrowing or rewarding experiences for the newly arrived parent. He has to deal with developing a relationship with a new partner, along with developing a parental relationship with youngsters going through a confusing and difficult time in their lives. The more children there are, the more trying the development of the blended family can be.

The new parent is often unsure of where he fits and how to act. As long as there is good communication between the partners and an understanding of what one can expect from the other, dealing with the children may be no more difficult than in initial families. Parents can relate to the children in any way that feels comfortable to them and that works.

Adolescents, by their nature, will test boundaries with the new parent. It is important these boundaries be established or reaffirmed soon and quickly—and as lovingly as possible. Trying to win over the children by being lenient can only lead to greater difficulties later. Children, especially adolescents, respect structure if is consistent and has a sense of fairness about it. New parents should not be afraid of setting limits, pending any legal or relationship constraints. It is important for parents to work together to focus on safe and supportive care for the children.

I was asked what the most important part of parenting is. After some thought, I responded, "Listen to them!"

EDUCATIONAL CONSIDERATIONS

Whatever the family unit is needs to be known by the school and its staff. Who has permission to take the child from school should be on the child's record and kept accessible.

In the case of blended families or single parents, it should be clear whether other adults can pick up the child. Signed permission should be done by the parent who has registered the child in the school or school district. It may be helpful to have a copy of the custody document to verify the situation.

As an elementary school principal, I remember getting a call from a family in which the children resided with their father and a step-mother. The caller informed us that the children's mother was coming in from another state and might try to take the children away. We were told the father had custody and under no circumstances should the children leave with the mother.

Sure enough, in mid-afternoon the mother arrived and announced she wanted her children. I explained to her we had instructions she did not have permission to take the children. (A court order would have helped here.)

She said she was going to get her children and began to walk down the hall. I asked her to come back to the office and told her I would call the sheriff if she continued.

The issue went to the local courts, and the mother was prohibited from getting within 50 feet of her children. She was told by the judge she faced jail if she did not comply. This is a difficult situation for the schools, but it involves the safety of the children, an obligation for all of the school staff.

Survival Tips

- Sharing household responsibilities is important for the youngster to be a part of the family.
- Allowance gives the youngster some freedom for independent spending decisions.
- Love your child unconditionally.
- If you blend a family, establish boundaries and expectations quickly and that are fair to everyone.
- School staff should know who has custody of the students and who else may have permission to remove them from the school campus.

REFERENCE

U.S. Census Bureau. (2018). *Families and living arrangements tables.* Available at: https://www.census.gov/newsroom/press-releases/2018/families.html, retrieved 15 March 2020.

Part II

FIRST DROP

5

Encouraging Adolescents to Be Accountable

"Wha'd'ya Mean It's My Responsibility?"

BEHAVIORS HAVE CONSEQUENCES

First, there is little a parent can *make* an adolescent do (Tobias, 2012). Most behavior is *encouraged* or *coerced* through a system of rewards (or punishments). These rewards can be tangible—for example, allowance or privileges—or intangible—for instance, love or respect.

Youngsters should be given the opportunity to make decisions that are rightly theirs to make and realize decision making carries with it *responsibility for action*. Some youngsters do not embrace personal responsibility.

Parents have the *power* to act as parents. The degree to which they are able to act effectively is a function of knowing how to communicate.

Parents have the *authority*, the right to act as parents. That right can be taken away if they are abusive or violent.

Parents have the *responsibility*, the obligation to act as parents. They are obliged to provide a safe (and loving) home for their children, adequate nourishment and nutrition, and a healthy environment.

Many parents attempt to control their children's lives—either by design or habit. When children reach adolescence, they begin to rebel against this control. If parents insist on one-sided control—not involving the youngster in decisions—it is not surprising constant battles erupt.

It is important that youngsters be given increasing responsibility for their decisions and held accountable for the results of those decisions (see Dreikurs & Grey, 1990). Nonetheless, children may not have ample skill in making decisions that affect them. Parents make the majority of their child's decisions, but they also *rescue* the child from bad decisions made by her.

Children should have the *ability* to decide about things in their lives, and the *situation* should be appropriate for them to decide. Not every child is able to make a decision, nor is every situation geared to the child's decision-making ability. As they enter adolescence, they begin to develop their abstract thinking ability, but they are not fully formed yet (see Epstein, 1990).

At an early age, about when children can truly begin to reason, they may be given *structured* decisions to make. *Not*: "What do you want for breakfast?" *Rather*: "Do you want cereal or eggs for breakfast?" In this way, when a child answers with an inappropriate response, for example, "pizza," you can respond with, "That is not one of the choices. You may have cereal or eggs or not have breakfast."

We know going without breakfast will leave the child short of energy during the morning, and we can share this information with the child: "If you don't eat breakfast, you will be hungry." He will not starve but eventually will realize that eating breakfast, choosing from available foods, will allow him not to be hungry.

Of course, if not eating breakfast is permissible for the parent, the child should not be allowed to eat until the next established mealtime. In that way, she will understand the consequences for his decision. The parent can say, "I'm sorry you're hungry, but you decided not to eat breakfast. You'll have to wait until lunch."

Parents worry children will make poor decisions, so they do not allow the child to make those that are hers. This is not to say a child should make every decision, especially those for which she does not have sufficient information or experience. She should have an increasing range of decision choices for which she is responsible (see Ginott, 1982).

Many times, the only decisions an adolescent makes is what to wear or whom to date. When this youngster graduates from high school and is asked what her plans are for the rest of her life, it may not be surprising when she does not have a concrete answer. The decision for the future may be one for which she is not prepared to make because she has not had sufficient experience or information with which to make such an important decision.

Decision making involves several basic steps.

1. Identifying the decision issue in sufficient detail.
2. Outlining the potential choices, with existing limitations.
3. Looking at the advantages and disadvantages of each choice.
4. Deciding which choice seems the best and putting it in place.
5. Evaluating if the choice has worked in the desired way.

The parent can help the child become an adept decision maker if the parent is willing to allow the child to make decisions and live with the consequences of her decisions.

WHY PHYSICAL PUNISHMENT DOESN'T WORK

The old adage of "Spare the rod and spoil the child" seems wrong in today's world (see Sege, 2018). Children are not spoiled simply because they are not beaten. The older the child, the more inappropriate spanking is. Physical punishment teaches the child two things:

1. My parent can hurt me.
2. If you're big enough, it's okay to hit.

These messages can allow the child to develop into a bully (see chapter 10) and an abuser. What happens is children begin to fear their parents, and that can get in the way of establishing the mutual respect necessary for successful parent–adolescent relationships.

Parents may demand respect but oftentimes do not give it in return to the adolescent. For example, the parent may insist on the youngster's knocking before entering the parent's room. Yet, the parent may enter the youngster's room without knocking. The outward evidence of respect—showing deference, not speaking unless spoken to, saying "Yes, sir" or "Yes, ma'am"—fall short of true respect, backed by love and caring.

Inconsistent behavior on the part of the parent can confuse the child and cause her to adopt inconsistent behavior patterns. Parents telling children not to smoke from the midst of the smoke-filled family room or spanking the child who has just hit her brother leave confusing messages in the mind of the child.

Inflicting physical pain teaches the youngster little more than to develop strategies to avoid that pain. This may cause the child to be secretive or dishonest. Moreover, it is difficult for a child to believe the parent who is spanking her loves him at that moment. In her mind, she may be saying, "How can you love me and beat me at the same time?"

Acknowledging that physical punishment hurts may be the first step to a parent's finding another strategy. The logical or natural consequences (Dreikurs & Grey, 1990) are usually more effective to guide the child to behave appropriately.

Problem: A son called his father's office one day to say he had overslept. He asked if his father could come home and take him to school; he was told "No" (an example of parental assertiveness, not rescuing the child from a responsibility that was his).

The youngster said he would stay home from school that day; he was a junior in high school at that time. He was told the choice was his, but if he did not go to school, he could not go out of state to play in a regional soccer tournament.

Of course, as most teenagers are accustomed to do, he asked why. His father told him the rules at home were the same as the rules for school: If you do not attend, you are not eligible to play.

He asked what he was to do. He was told the choice was his. (This is an appropriate response for an experienced youngster; less experienced children might be provided with a list of possibilities as seen by the parent.) The problem was placed squarely where it belonged—on his shoulders.

Possible Solution: The youngster could call a ride service (presuming he had access to a ride-service account), a little poorer but a lot wiser. He could then go to the soccer tournament and have an exciting weekend. [If there were not a ready source of money, he probably would have to make the long walk to school or call a friend. He would probably not forego the soccer weekend.]

Other more traditional options for the father in this situation might have been the following:

1. Leave work and take the boy to school (of course, this imposes on the parent's workday and may cause problems there)
2. Punish the youngster because he failed to take care of his responsibility to get up on time and go to school (this may be arbitrary and unduly punitive)
3. Ignore the lack of responsibility and allow the boy go to the soccer tournament, even though he had not gone to school

(this reinforces the idea responsibilities may be shirked and there are no consequences for shirked responsibilities)
4. Spank the youngster for failing to get up on time and get to school

The expectations and consequences were clear, and because of this, the youngster had clear options: "Whether I go to the soccer tournament depends on the decision I make."

The idea of making decisions and accepting consequences brings a specific issue into the discussion: Who is responsible for the youngster's bedtime and getting the youngster up for school?

In adolescence, these responsibilities are the youngster's. Going to bed too late usually means being tired the next day. Lying in bed too long usually means missing the bus or being late to school. (Of course, the parent should provide a working alarm for each youngster.)

Missing the bus means the youngster has to find an alternate way of getting to school. If the parents have not left for work and they are willing to provide transportation, they can do so. However, there may be a nominal transportation fee, which is deducted from allowance (more about this later). If neither parent is home, then the youngster has to become creative, because missing school is not a permissible option. (It also may be in violation of the compulsory attendance law in many states.)

Physical punishment does not work, especially for adolescents. It may be an expression of irrational anger and may copy what the parent experienced when she was a youngster.

Further, physical punishment for adolescents is humiliating and can severely damage the parent–teen relationship. There is also the risk the youngster may retaliate, if she thinks she can win a physical struggle, which may make the situation wholly intolerable.

Adolescents can try the patience of their parents but tend to be reasonable individuals, if they are given the chance to be so. Part of this reason is the expectation by the parents that the youngster will act responsibly and can do so.

WHAT'S "DIS" ALL ABOUT?

In the common language of youngsters, "dissing" means disrespecting someone. The older a child gets, the more this may incite him. There seem to be five kinds of "dis":

Dis-respect

Dis-obedience

Dis-regard (or dismissiveness)

Dis-agreement

Discipline

The hyphenated words separate the negative from the positive (respect, obedience, regard, and agreement). We will talk more about discipline as a separate idea.

What is permissible for a child to do? If we accept children as individuals and entitled to their own thoughts and opinions, then they are entitled to have different ideas and beliefs than we do. They may *disagree* with us. That is okay! Again: That is okay! Talking about the different perspectives may be a way for parents and children to understand one another better.

Our children may resemble us physically and in other ways, but they are entitled to be themselves. They do not need our permission to be themselves. If we try to control their thoughts and beliefs, they will surely rebel at some point, especially if control challenges who they are (or think they are).

While it may chafe the parent, let us start with, "It is okay if you disagree with me." That leads to the *nonnegotiable* boundaries—what is not okay. "It is not okay for you to disobey, disrespect, or disregard me." (See Rosemond [n.d.] for additional discussion of these notions.)

Children are entitled to be themselves, and they may be different from us. They may even express opposing perspectives. What they are not permitted to do is be disrespectful or disobedient. Within reason, they must do what we say, and they may not demean us or be discourteous (another "dis"?) to others.

Furthermore, they may not disregard us. This may be another form of disobedience, or it may simply be ignoring us: "Oh, were you talking to me?" or "I didn't hear you say that." (See chapter 12, "Listening to Your Adolescent," on verifying understanding of messages.)

What most of us want is *discipline*. For many of us, we have to do something *to* the youngster. Rather, this means the youngster knows what to do that is right, correct, and appropriate, and will make the proper decision to do those things.

Where we enter the picture is if the youngster makes the wrong decision. Some might say we *discipline* the child. We offer guidance to a better decision.

Discipline is the pattern of behavior a child *chooses*. If that pattern "follows the rules," few problems arise. If the child seems undisciplined (that is, breaks the rules), then we step in and try to redirect the child.

We *invite* the child (through reason or threatened punishment) to change. Sometimes we are successful, and sometimes we are not. In either case, the child chooses. This means she decides how to behave. She *disciplines* herself.

Her defiance to test the boundaries may be a function of her strong will (cf. Tobias, 2012). Coming to an agreement may occur when she gets her needs (not her *wants*) met and is motivated to be in an OK place (see chapter 13 for more).

TURNING LOOSE

When is the *right* time to turn loose, to allow the child to become more or totally responsible for her decisions? Two things should be considered—1) the comfort level of the parent and 2) the readiness of the child. (Note: Readiness may be connected with age, but chronology may be very different from emotional or conceptual maturity.)

While it is easy to say the child should make decisions that are rightly hers to make, it is another thing to come to grips with reality. This means the parent has reasonable assurance that this decision making is appropriate at this time in the child's life.

It means not rescuing children from poor decisions, *excluding* those that may be physically harmful. Parents may know, or think they know, what the outcomes of certain decisions are and may even share that knowledge with the child, but ultimately the decision is the child's. She will have to live with the consequences.

Such issues as dating, dress, car ownership/privileges, hairstyle, bedtime, and eating patterns are among some of the most common arenas for battles between parents and adolescents. "You are not going to date until you're sixteen. My parents wouldn't let me date, and I'm not going to let you."

Our own history as adolescents tends to drive many of the decisions we make, or try to make, for our own children. Our history as youngsters carries us into our own parenthood.

As much as we rebelled as teenagers, we still imbue many of our parents' values as our own. We need to be aware of a certain degree of fairness and current fashion and trends.

Another example: One issue may be a youngster's hairstyle. Typically, most parents will accompany their youngster to the haircutter and give directions for the cut.

Problem: One day a teenager was left at the haircutter by herself. She came home with a style her parents felt was uncomplimentary and too bizarre for their taste. The parents had paid for the haircut and felt betrayed she would decide on such a radical style.

Possible Solutions: Confront the situation by telling the youngster they did not like her decision, but also acknowledge it was her decision. Since it is her hair, she could decide on the style.

However, tell her if they did not approve beforehand, she would have to pay for the haircut herself.

At first, she would likely object, but she would see she has control of the way she looks. She will have to live with the consequences of the decision.

If her friends laugh, she will have to endure that embarrassment. You might tell her others do judge people by the way they look, and she might impress her teachers or a potential employer negatively.

Having all of the information, she needs to make the decision. It is hers to make. (Her personality may be a major factor in decisions of how she looks. See chapter 13, "Communicating with Your Adolescent.")

Your level of comfort is reached by examining the way you feel—about having paid for a haircut that did not meet with your approval, by acknowledging how much control you should exercise, and by realizing who has to live with the results of the decision. After considering all of these aspects, you will realize you are only observers of the situation.

You are interested in the outcome. You do not want her to be hurt, but you really do not need to do more than provide the necessary information about possible outcomes. After all, your friends are not going to laugh at you, and you are not likely to be disregarded for a possible job.

Allowing youngsters to make their own decisions, within boundaries of safety, is a crucial part of growing into adulthood. This includes living with the consequences of those decisions (see Rosemond, 1998).

The following is a note to an adolescent leaving for college. It reminds her about boundaries and limits regarding financial support. More importantly, it reminds her of her responsibilities.

Dearest daughter,

Just so you understand where the money for your college expenses comes from: We put money away for your education. Unfortunately, what your mother and I could afford was not enough for all of your expenses. You were told what you could expect when you were in high school. You were also told that it would probably not be enough and that you would have to find another way to make up the difference—scholarships, work, loans, etc.

I am very pleased at your accepting some of the responsibility by working. While I know it has not always been pleasant, it has given you some sense of accomplishment. I hope you will consider taking a course load so that your allowance runs out at the same time you complete your degree.

The money we put aside for you is in an annuity—a fund that distributes part of the proceeds on a yearly basis. That distribution does not come until the end of August. As a result, any money that you need before the end of August must come from other sources. We have taken care of that as best we can. I am glad that we have been able to help. You should be prepared and not expect "instant loans" or other rescues. While I understand your wanting to take off to relax or to shop, you should be sure you have taken care of your anticipated obligations—rent, food, etc. In that way, you will not have to call for us to "bail you out."

You have grown into a lovely person. I am proud of what you have become and what you have accomplished. I am also excited at the potential I expect you will fulfill as a professional—in whatever field you choose. You are very capable, and I know you have begun to realize how capable you are.

If you have any questions or need our help in coming up with a plan, will you ask us?

EDUCATIONAL CONSIDERATIONS

School may be an extension of the home in many ways. Children learn from trained staff and as dictated by educational authorities. These students may have little or no input regarding the curriculum or how it is presented.

In some states, it may still be legal for schools to use corporal punishment. Parents should know whether this practice is used in their child's school. They may choose to object to its use and ask to be called before their child is spanked.

With increasing violence in schools, school safety officers may be present. It is their job to be a deterrent to altercations between students. They may also be the first line of defense should danger present from outside.

For the most part, students are a captive audience. Their schedule is prescribed, and their teachers are assigned. Other than a choice of elective courses, they may not be involved in their educational choices.

Classrooms are usually arranged according to the teacher's preferences. Instructional delivery is also the teacher's, sometimes without regard for student learning styles.

Students are expected to acquiesce to what is presented and obey their teachers and the student handbook. For adolescent students, pushback against rules and formats may become more prevalent than before.

Outcomes are the evidence of what students have learned. They are usually measured by standardized tests and grade-point averages. Criteria for the former are normed to a larger population. Criteria for the latter are established by the teachers.

Grades can be problematic. They may be seen as student ability to meet teacher expectations. Moreover, students whose learning preferences are different from instructional delivery may not perform as well as their counterparts whose preferences are more closely aligned with their teacher's (Gilbert, 2014, 2018).

(Note: Meeting teacher expectations may or may not indicate academic growth. High school graduates may arrive at colleges and universities incompletely prepared for higher-education academics, even if they may have had acceptable grade-point averages to be admitted [see Gilbert, 2000].)

The key to academic performance is connecting with students in ways they prefer, as much as possible (Bradley, Pauley, & Pauley, 2006; Gilbert, 2012; Pauley, Bradley, & Pauley, 2002). Failure to connect effectively can lead to predictable negative behaviors that can result in students being removed from the learning situation. Missing important information and lessons can result in poor performance.

Survival Tip

- Children should make decisions that are rightly theirs to make.
- Parents should be wary of rescuing their children from poor decisions.
- Spanking is physically abusive and teaches children to be abusive.
- Mutual respect is important as children are held accountable for their decisions.
- Connecting with all students effectively is the foundation for acceptable academic performances

---

REFERENCES

Bradley, D., Pauley, J. A., &. Pauley, J. F. (2006). *Effective classroom management: Six keys to success.* Lanham, MD: Rowman & Littlefield.

Dreikurs, R., & Grey, L. (1990). *Logical consequences: A new approach to discipline.* New York: Dutton.

Epstein, H. T. (1990). Stages in human mental growth. *Journal of Educational Psychology, 82*(4): 876–80.

Gilbert, M. B. (2000). An analysis of factors related to school-district size in Arkansas. *Research in the Schools, 7*(2): 31–37.

Gilbert, M. B. (2012). *Communicating effectively: Tools for educational leaders* (2nd ed.). Lanham, MD: Rowman & Littlefield.

Gilbert, M. B. (2014). Different strokes for different folks: Connecting with students for academic success. *International Journal of Education, 6*(4): 1–13. Available at: http://www.macrothink.org/journal/index.php/ije/article/view/6269/5313, retrieved 15 March 2020.

Gilbert, M. B. (2018). Student performance is linked to connecting effectively with teachers. *Journal of Research in Innovative Teaching and Learning, 12*(1): 311–24, https://doi.org/10.1108/JRIT-05-2018-0010.

Ginott, H. (1982). *Between parent and teenager.* New York: HarperCollins.

Pauley, J. A., Bradley, D., & Pauley, J. F. (2002). *Here's how to reach me: Matching instruction to personality types in your classroom.* Baltimore, MD: Paul H. Brookes.

Rosemond, J. (n.d.) *Been there done that! The teenage years made simple (sorta)* [audiotape]. Gastonia, NC: Center for Affirmative Parenting.

Rosemond, J. (1998). *Teen-proofing: Fostering responsible decision-making in your teenager.* Kansas City, MO: Andrews McMeel.

Sege, R. D. (2018, November 5). AAP policy opposes corporal punishment, draws on recent evidence. *AAP News.* Available at: https://www.aappublications.org/news/2018/11/05/discipline110518, retrieved 15 March 2020.

Tobias, C. U. (2012). *You can't make me (but I can be persuaded): Strategies for bringing out the best in your strong-willed child* (Rev. ed.). Colorado Springs, CO: WaterBrook Press.

The Importance of Having Friends

As tweenagers become teenagers, their burgeoning independence moves them outside the home more and more. They seek the company of peers who will help to develop their individuality and autonomy. They *need* companionship.

If they have moved to a new school, forming new friendships can be as awkward and difficult as adjusting to their new bodies. What criteria do they use?

What is a friend? Someone they can trust. Someone who likes the same things they do. Someone who accepts them for who they are.

Adolescents need relationships with others who share common interests (Rice & Dolgin, 2008). They need others who will stand beside them in a caring and understanding way. They will be a support for one another.

When I was a preadolescent, I had two chums. We shared common interests and generally enjoyed one another's company. Every Friday night we would meet in someone's home to watch

our favorite TV show and share potato chips, pretzels, and pea-
nuts in the shell. It was a relatively brief encounter, but I think we
all looked forward to it.

I do not remember much more than sharing time together. It
was pleasant.

I wonder where they are today.

CAN WE HELP?

Kids take their cues from one another. As parents, we hope these are
positive.

The issue is we can only *hope*. We cannot choose the company our
adolescents keep. Moreover, they do not want our interference.

What we can do is provide them with the values and information to
make good choices. We provide a home. We choose the religious affilia-
tion and congregation, if we want organized religion in the family's life.
We set (and *practice*) rules for decorum, etiquette and acceptable social
interaction. Again, we *hope* this is enough for our children to assert
positive influences on their lives.

While adolescents want more and more independence, it is hard to
loosen the parental reins. We want to know where our kids are, what
they are doing and with whom, and when they will be home.

A recent commercial for cell phones focused on a family with
six children. Each used the phone differently—gaming, video
chatting, texting, etc. One was taking flying lessons to become a
pilot. The tag at the end is, "When he lands, he knows he needs
to call Mama."

We want to know our children are safe at all times. Getting to a point of comfort when they are out of our sight and influence can be challenging.

If our children trust us and understand our wanting to be involved in their lives, they will stay in touch. If we are overbearing and insist on controlling what they do, they may resist our involvement and be secretive.

Real versus Virtual Friends

Helping our teens make good (according to us) decisions regarding the selection of their friends may not be what we do beforehand. We tend to judge their friends after we know who they are.

We need to talk with our children at pivotal junctures in their lives (adolescence onset, school change, etc.) about what to expect and how to negotiate the shoals and pitfalls—or to continue the analogy, to be sure their safety belts are fastened so they don't fall off the roller coaster.

Their expanding interaction circles usually start close to home—neighborhood, congregation, sport teams, organizations (scouts, youth groups, etc.). Of course, school provides a pool of potential friends.

Before and into early adolescence, friends tend to be of the same gender. The criteria expand as the children grow older to include common interests, as well as those of other genders.

A burgeoning pool of potential friends may be found online in social media. We have the ability to restrict or monitor use as our children have their own electronic devices.

Having a working mobile phone may be helpful in staying in touch with our children. We should take full advantage of parental controls as we allow our children to have phones and other electronic devices.

Social media are quite enticing to curious minds, aside from e-mail and texting. Our children are beginning to develop social filters but still may be naïve and too trusting.

Parents should be aware of the dangers that confront all of us in the anonymity and possible duplicity one can encounter in cyberspace.

We need to limit what access they have to internet sites and applications, especially as they are maturing.

Face-to-face (FtF) social interactions enhance well-being (Shakya & Nicholas, 2017). Substituting virtual friends for real ones can stunt the development of social skills and the ability to interact with others effectively in everyday, real-world settings.

Virtual friends are no substitute for real ones. A majority of people tend to be happier when talking with a friend FtF. Social networking is convenient for keeping in touch, especially with those who are not readily accessible. Real connections are best when we can experience friendship in person. Virtual friendships do not prepare use for real social interactions. We can avoid bonding and hide personal flaws. True friends accept us for who we are, "warts and all." This is accomplished best when we can experience each other FtF (Antao, 2013).

Guidelines for Electronic Interaction

We can be both permissive and cautious as the electronic world opens for our children. Give them age-appropriate access but guide them accordingly, especially with regard to people they may meet online.

Talk with them about being careful about revealing too much of their personal information with people they do not know. This includes home address, phone number, e-mail address, and pictures. You may want to observe their initial encounters and redirect them, if necessary.

As they become more sophisticated with their interactions and you become more comfortable, you can back away. However, remind your youngsters you are always available if they have questions or are confused about what to do or say online. (Trust underpins your being a resource.)

EDUCATIONAL CONSIDERATIONS

As children move into adolescence, they are likely to experience a change of the organization of the school. They will transition from a mostly self-contained setting at the elementary level to increasing departmentalization at the middle/junior high and high school. They are beginning to be thrust into environments that demand increasing self-sufficiency.

Having close relationships with one or two people can help the youngster cope with the academic, physical, social, and emotional changes. Navigating everything that is going on can be daunting.

Schools designed to accommodate the changes may reduce the problems. Having teaching and support staffs with the necessary specialized training and understanding of adolescence is imperative.

While imparting the *content* of the curriculum, the conceptual "copartner" of *connecting effectively* must be considered. Not all learners respond equally to the same instructional delivery. Differences in performance are linked significantly to communication matches/mismatches between teacher and students (cf. Gilbert, 2013, 2014, 2018).

Having access to a computer may be an important part of the school curriculum. Some instruction may be offered, and some schoolwork may be completed electronically. Electronic connection may also allow us to monitor our youngster's progress.

Electronic devices can be wonderful adjuncts for teaching; however, personal interaction between teachers and students is imperative for both academic and social growth.

I was surprised recently when I received an e-mail from a former student. I never expected I had impressed the individual to the point where he wanted to reach out fifty years after graduation. He spoke of how he respected what I knew and how I taught. He is now a retired orthodontist. We met for a very pleasant catching up. One never knows.

Having friends is important for growth and well-being.

Survival Tips

- Suggest criteria for choosing friends.
- From increasingly farther distance, oversee relationships youngsters have with others.
- Respect decisions regarding friends unless there is a reason to intervene.
- Connect with school regarding their programs, both academic and ancillary.
- Use electronic devices to supplement human interaction and be wary of their uses.

REFERENCES

Antao, L. (2013, May 12). Virtual vs. real friends. *E Times.* Available at: https://timesofindia.indiatimes.com/life-style/relationships/love-sex/Virtual-vs-real-friends/articleshow/19740338.cms, retrieved 16 January 2020.

Gilbert, M. B. (2013). A plea for systemic change in education. *On the Horizon, 21*(4): 312–22.

Gilbert, M. B. (2014). Different strokes for different folks: Connecting with students for academic success. *International Journal of Education, 6*(4): 119–31, https://doi:10.5296/ije.v6i4.6269.

Gilbert, M. B. (2018). Student performance is linked to connecting effectively with teachers. *Journal of Research of Innovation in Teaching and Learning, 12*(3): 311–24, https://doi.org/10.1108/JRIT-05-2018-0010.

Rice, F. P., & Dolgin, K. G. (2008). *The adolescent: Development, relationships and culture* (12th ed.). Upper Saddle River, NJ: Pearson.

Shakya, H. B., & Christakis, N. A. (2017). Association of Facebook with compromised well-being: A longitudinal study. *American Journal of Epidemiology, 185*(3): 203–11, https://doi.org/10.1093/aje/kww189.

Part III

LOOP-DE-LOOP

Adolescents in Cyberspace

When exploring outer space became an exciting reality, we wanted to know what was/is out there. We became curiouser and curiouser (with apologies to Lewis Carroll and the Cheshire Cat).

With the advent of the internet, we now have the ability to explore cyberspace. It is intriguing, exciting, mind-expanding, and potentially dangerous.

Our adolescents are no less curious than adults. We all must be aware of the dangers and cyber-traps (see later in this chapter).

Having access to a computer may be mandatory for instructional reasons and to have a connection with the school. Parents should determine whether the school has adequate safety procedures in place to protect youngsters.

One of the increasing dangers is the amount of time teens spend on-line. Social media and gaming are the main activities, aside from e-mail and texting. Our children are beginning to develop social filters but are still naïve and trusting.

DANGERS

Parents should be aware of the dangers in cyberspace. Having electronic access (mobile phones, smartphones, etc.) to our children and them to us is important. But we need to limit what access they have to internet sites and applications, especially as they are maturing.

Cyberbullying: Youngsters can fall victim to an incessant online attack, turning a game or interchange into real or virtual humiliation (see chapter 10).

Cyberpredators: Adolescents can be vulnerable to individuals who try to take advantage of others for personal or sexual reasons. They lurk on social media looking for opportunities to exploit innocence or naïveté.

Posting private information: Uninitiated users may not understand social boundaries. Youngsters are developing their filters but need guidance. Their social media profiles should not be public.

Phishing: E-mails can be used to trick youngsters into clicking on malicious links or attachments. (Using similar tricks in texts is called *smishing.*)

Scams: Youngsters may visit popular sites that identify potential victims for promising "prizes." To claim the reward, people need to provide a processing fee via access to payment information. Youngsters are still learning to be wary, as are adults.

Malware: Software designed to perform harmful actions on your computer can steal personal information or hijack your computer via phishing. Sometimes hijackers will lock out the user and demand ransom. No one should download software without first checking its authenticity by going directly to the website of the application without using a provided link. One should perform periodic checks for computer integrity and lack of corrupted files.

Haunting Posts: There is no *delete* key on the internet. Anything put online can be almost impossible to remove. Teens grow up and can be embarrassed by what they thought was cute or funny to post when they were younger. Colleges and businesses can check the background of youngsters as they apply for admission or a job. Advise your kids to think carefully about whether they want what they post available to everyone. (Kaspersky Lab, 2020)

> I remember seeing a particularly nasty interchange between a mother and daughter on social media. I wondered whether they wanted everyone to view their disagreement and, if so, why.

The important guidance is to beware of the dangers and pitfalls of being in cyberspace. Counsel your children before they "blast off."

The following safety tips are for your consideration. Some might appeal to you; others may seem overly intrusive. Collaborate with your teen to set rules. Doing this will assure trust, as you test your own limits.

Safety Tips

1. Communicate to your kids that digital devices deserve respect. Have them ask for permission in the same way they might ask permission to go out or to someone's home.
2. Consider setting rules on when and where your kids have access to devices or specific apps. Using their devices in common areas may give you an opportunity to monitor what they are viewing.
3. Create a schedule so kids are using their devices during periods when you can provide the most oversight. Again, you are looking for safe use.
4. Consider a technology agreement for each child. This will put your common understanding in writing. It is a contract. If it is broken, you can decide the consequences to be enforced.
5. Be sure to talk with your kids about privacy—or lack thereof—and tone. The key here is that teens understand that their online presence

may not be as private as they think. Their electronic footprint may be indelible.

6. Take some time to think about what you're comfortable—and uncomfortable—with your kids doing online. Again, the keys are safety and trust.

7. It might be time to talk about pornography. Teens probably understand, in general terms, what pornography is. However, you may want to reassure yourself that they know what they should and should not view. You might say, "You should tell me if you ever see that stuff, not because I'd be mad at you or you've done anything wrong, but just because I want you to know how to make your computer safer so that doesn't happen again" (Dr. Emily Rothman, community health scientist at Boston University School of Public Health).

8. And remember, kids will be kids, including when they're online. They continue to be curious. They will test boundaries. In the end, your guidance will give them the information they need for the decisions they make. (adapted from Moyer, 2020)

Suggestions

As mentioned in the previous chapter, face-to-face (FtF) social interactions enhance well-being (Shakya & Nicholas, 2017). Substituting virtual friends for real ones can stunt the development of social skills and the ability to interact with others effectively in everyday, real-world settings.

While connecting electronically is relatively easy, it may breed an overconfidence we are communicating effectively because we are connected. It is difficult to convey emotion and tone without the accompanying paralinguistic cues of gesture, emphasis, and intonation (Kruger, Epley, Parker, & Ng, 2005).

We have developed some shortcuts to help—emojis/emoticons to simulate emotions, all caps to indicate emphasis or anger, etc. Missing are the human aspects of communication—eye contact, body language, and other visual cues.

Some applications that allow a video connection may help, but there is something still missing. The FtF contact can help as we try to gain an understanding of what the message is.

Caution: Too much screen time has been linked to anxiety and depression in teens (Twenge & Campbell, 2018). Structuring the use of electronic devices is important to keeping children safe. Some outcomes of too much screen time are as follows:

Lower psychological well-being

More excitability and less self-control

Lower task completion

Lessened curiosity in learning new things (Boers, Afzali, & Newton, 2019)

These data are alarming and suggest careful monitoring. The world has changed for parents and their children. The following are some guidelines:

Set limits. Limit the time your kids spend online. Be knowledgeable about the applications and websites your children are using and what information they're accessing online. Screen time should not equal alone time. Engage with your children when they are using screens. Offer to watch their television shows or play their video games. This way their screen time becomes a more social event, where you have the chance to discuss the content. Technology should not be a reward. Screens are an easy way to calm your child or keep them quiet, but pacifying them with media is forming a very bad habit. Children should learn how to handle their emotions and manage boredom without the aid of a screen. (Reducing or eliminating screen time can be a consequence of misbehavior.)

Find a balance. Kids will inevitably interact with screens as more schools provide children with tablets and computers in the classroom. As the need for screen time increases, set a good example and teach your kids about the importance of privacy and the dangers of predators and sexting.

Listen to your kids. Ask your children how they respond to the digital content they consume. Remind them that what they see online is not an accurate measure of reality—for example, someone may have taken thirty photos to post one "candid" shot. (adapted from the American Academy of Pediatrics, 2018)

EDUCATIONAL CONSIDERATIONS

The internet provides a wealth of available resources from the comfort of home or other relaxed environment. It is rarer today for students to need to roam the stacks of library books or try to find information in a heavy-book encyclopedia.

Schools can take advantage of this huge trove of information. Assignments can be more extensive, knowing there are available resources.

The same cautions prevail as with social media, with some additions. Students should be alerted to check the veracity of the sources. Not everything on the internet is necessarily true or presented objectively.

School-related use of the internet by students may include the following:

Student research

Major source for a school project

Use of school- or class-based websites

Study aids

Creation of a web page for a school project (Simon, Graziano, & Lenhart, 2001)

Additionally, schools may use online instruction as a surrogate for FtF instruction. With the coronavirus scare (2020), many schools cancelled classes to prevent the potential interpersonal contact of spreading disease. Instead, they went to electronic interaction.

As schools rely more on the internet for legitimate activities, they should be aware of potential misuse. Legitimate use includes the internet as a teaching tool (providing information, group projects, etc.), instant messaging as a homework helper, tutoring, prepping for standardized tests (SAT, ACT, etc.), and websites about school or classes.

Using resource checkers from time to time to be sure student papers are original may be necessary. Pirated papers (sometimes for a price) and other sources to be plagiarized lurk on the internet.

Students should be encouraged to use available resources but warned of inappropriate use. As with embarrassing posts, cheating can follow students and damage reputations.

Other than misuse, schools should have guidelines for screen time. Overuse can lead to cognitive and physical problems (National Education Policy Center, 2020).

Survival Tips

- The internet is pervasive in today's world.
- Be aware of the dangers for yourself and, especially, your youngsters.
- Talk about guidelines for use (appropriate posting, screen time, etc.).
- Be a resource/friendly critic for profiles your teen wants to post.
- Find available resources to report predatory and other dangerous behavior.
- Check with the school to see how they use the internet and protect student use.

REFERENCES

American Academy of Pediatrics. (2018). Media and children communication toolkit. *American Academy of Pediatrics.* Available at: https://www.aap.org/en-us/about-the-aap/aap-press-room/news-features-and-safety-tips/Pages/Children-and-Media-Tips.aspx, retrieved 9 January 2020.

Boers, E., Afzali, M. H., & Newton, N. (2019). Association of screen time and depression in adolescence. *JAMA Pediatrics, 173*(9), 853–59, https://doi:10.1001/jamapediatrics.2019.1759.

Kaspersky Lab. (2020). Internet safety for kids: How to protect your children from the top seven dangers they face online. *Kaspersky.* Available at: https://usa.kaspersky.com/resource-center/threats/top-seven-dangers-children-face-online, retrieved 20 January 2020.

Kruger, J., Epley, N., Parker, J., & Ng, Z.-W. (2005). Egocentrism over e-mail: Can we communicate as well as we think? *Journal of Personality and Social Psychology, 89*(6): 925–36.

National Educational Policy Center (NEPC). (2020, February 20). Misuse of screens in schools: An action kit to help parents. *NEPC Newsletter.* Available at: http://www.icontact-archive.com/archive?c=1748247&f=3100&s=3172&m=147127&t=683ff6e55fceb8d669aa5ea6b8253ac84d14528c98c4873195440427f0ff88d5, retrieved 20 February 2020.

Moyer, M. W. (2020, April 2). Teaching your kids to be safe online: A hasty primer. *New York Times.* Available at: https://www.nytimes.com/2020/04/02/parenting/coronavirus-children-online-etiquette.html?refrringSource=articleShare, retrieved 4 April 2020.

Shakya, H. B., & Christakis, N. A. (2017). Association of Facebook with compromised well-being: A longitudinal study. *American Journal of Epidemiology, 185*(3): 203–11, https://doi.org/10.1093/aje/kww189.

Simon, M., Graziano, M., & Lenhart, A. (2001, September 1). The internet and education. *Pew Research Center.* Available at: https://www.pewresearch.org/internet/2001/09/01/the-internet-and-education/, retrieved 20 January 2020.

Twenge, M. J., & Campbell, W. K. (2018). Associations between screen time and lower psychological well-being among children and adolescents: Evidence from population-based study. *Preventive Medicine Reports, 12*(271): 271–83, https://doi.org/10.1016/j.pmedr.2018.10.003.

Part IV

CLIMBING

8

Activities for Adolescents

Aside from academics and being online, adolescents need productive and involving outlets for their energy and interests. Positive physical and social activities support their growing bodies and expanding minds.

As youngsters move away from the shelter of home into an expanding world of experience, they need to develop social skills. Guidance from parents, caregivers, and teachers is requisite. These skills include the following:

Listening. Being able to understand what people are saying by concentrating on the verbal message with undivided attention. (See also chapter 12.)

Assertiveness. The ability to express directly and confidently our genuine opinions, feelings, or attitudes, for example, that the rights of others and social circumstances are respected.

Emotional self-awareness. Getting in touch with emotions and raising awareness of how a particular emotion manifests itself, and how it affects life.

Understanding nonverbal communication. Basic nonverbal aspects of human behavior, including eye contact, tone of voice, facial expressions, gestures, personal distance, body language, and posture. (adapted from Nobel Coaching, 2017)

Practice in these skills will allow the adolescent to shed some of the awkwardness of more sophisticated social interaction. Part of the problem is rate of maturity.

Some develop faster than others. Those who develop more slowly can be ignored or shunned because they seem immature.

Pecking orders are important to teens. Empathy and compassion for those who are smaller or less adept are usually not high on the list of skills needed to thrive and survive. (Note: It will become more important later in life.)

STOKING THE FURNACE

Preteens and teens need physical activity regularly. Being active provides the following health benefits:

Improves heart and lung health

Boosts the immune system

Develops strong bones and muscles, and good posture

Helps to maintain a healthy weight and avoid being overweight

Reduces the risk of high blood pressure and anxiety (Australian Parenting Website, 2018)

Growing adolescent bodies burn lots of calories. The intake of food is amazing. When you are told young swimmers may consume 10,000 calories a day, you may think, "If I ate 10,000 calories a day, I would twice the person I am."

Of course, adult bodies have adjusted metabolisms. They no longer need to grow; hence, they need fewer calories.

Be careful of imposing your habits, regimens, or issues on your adolescent. Body image is a big deal. Don't bequeath them your issues

(Sole-Smith, 2020). If you struggle with your weight or looking as you would prefer, don't set that as an example for your growing teen.

They are still forming. Encourage them to eat healthy and exercise regularly. Affirm the positive actions they take.

The other part of that equation is how to burn calories. Adolescents need physical activity. What type of activity is recommended? Here are some guidelines from the Centers for Disease Control and Prevention (2020):

Aerobic Activity: Most of your child's daily 60 minutes of physical activity should be aerobic activities like walking, running, or anything that makes their hearts beat faster. In addition, encourage them to do aerobic activities at least three days a week that make them breathe fast and their hearts pound.

Muscle-Strengthening: Include such muscle-strengthening activities as climbing or doing push-ups at least three days per week as part of your child's daily 60 minutes or more.

Bone-Strengthening: Include bone-strengthening activities like jumping or running at least three days per week as part of your child's daily 60 minutes or more.

Physical activity is also great for the following:

Breaking up long periods of sitting or studying

Improving concentration and memory

Learning new skills

Increasing self-confidence

Reducing stress and improving sleep

Making and keeping friends (Australian Parenting Website, 2018)

PLACES FOR ACTIVITIES

Since energy levels of adolescents wax and wane during the day, having a schedule to exercise helps, but it requires self-motivation. Exercising with others works well for most teens. Sports, competitive or otherwise, provide superb outlets. The where is less important than the frequency.

ORGANIZED ACTIVITIES

School and church organizations are the likely sources of activities for teens. Sports teams are high on the list. Clubs and service groups are also positive outlets.

Being a competitive athlete can be ego-boosting and helpful for growth. In many communities, high school athletics are prominent in the lives of the citizens. Successful athletes can be "heroes."

Be sure to talk with your children about fleeting celebrity. Excellence can open to doors to scholarships and other opportunities. However, it is important to balance extracurricular excellence with success as a student.

Regardless of success, adolescents should be encouraged to participate in whatever physical activity intrigues them. Having a physical outlet later in life is good for physical and mental health.

Exercising with your teen is great for cementing your relationship. Parents should be careful of fulfilling their dreams through their children. Positive support is great for bonding. Undue criticism can be damaging.

One dangerous sidelight is *hazing* as entry into the culture of a team or club. Parents should stay vigilant as their teens become active on a team or in a club. If their behavior changes negatively, probe deeply for the reason.

Report any hazing or taunting to the proper authorities as soon as it is noticed. Teens will be reluctant to be forthcoming because of the possibility of being ostracized, but their safety is of paramount importance.

Competitive athletics predominate in today's culture. If your children have aptitude in other areas, for instance, art and performance, they should be encouraged and supported.

Additionally, service might also be considered. Volunteering in the community with agencies that appeal to the youngster should also be considered.

I was a proud grandparent when one of my grandsons talked eloquently about why he chose to help with projects to house and feed homeless people and families. He regaled those present at his 13th birthday celebration and asked that any cash presents be donated to the organization with which he was working.

SUCCESS AND FAILURE

The emphasis for most children (and later when they become adults) is the impetus to succeed. This emphasis can be either intrinsic (coming from internal sources) or extrinsic (coming from external sources—for example, parents, teachers, peers, etc.).

What is missing is permission to fail. Failure may be related by others to intelligence or expectations (Haimovitz & Dweck, 2016).

Success can be seen as being smart. We triumph when we succeed; we are smart because we have succeeded.

When we do not succeed, we (and others) may think it is because we are *not* smart. Our failure can be linked to our intelligence or lack thereof (Grose, 2020).

This notion is hard for the delicate egos of adolescents.

Success = smart/talented/adept
Failure = dumb/stupid/ignorant (or some other pejorative label)

Not succeeding opens the door to examine why and what to do next. If we were successful all of the time, it would be hard to develop new skills because the ones in place were working.

Help youngsters learn from their "failures." These life lessons may be important.

EDUCATIONAL CONSIDERATIONS

How high should the bar be when we teach? If everyone succeeds, then maybe we have not asked difficult enough questions. Of course, if we set the criteria for performance, we expect students to meet our expectations. Those whose learning styles are more in line with our teaching styles will do better than those whose learning preferences are different (Gilbert, 2013, 2014, 2018).

Whatever we choose, the curriculum to entail must be a precursor to the next level—subject matter, conceptual ability, or level of difficulty. If students are college-bound, the curriculum should prepare them adequately for higher-level learning. An adjunct to the curriculum is developing study skills.

College seems to be preferred as the next educational step. If students choose not to go to college, then they should be prepared for whatever is next—vocational training, military service, or job entry. All are appropriate.

Students must maintain satisfactory classroom performance to participate in extracurricular activities. Learning should be the higher priority, even though it may not have the same status as excelling in a sport.

Classroom teachers should partner with coaches and club sponsors to work in the best interests of the students. Undue pressure for missing school or assignments in deference to schedules of teams or clubs is inappropriate. School officials should plan for acceptable participation in both academic and other school-related activities.

Survival Tips

- Physical and social activities are important parts of adolescent growth.
- Screen time does not substitute for being physically active.
- Academics should be a higher priority than extracurricular activities.
- Interpret a child's successes (and failures) as theirs, not a reflection of others or your own. Their aspirations should be supported.

REFERENCES

Australian Parenting Website. (2018). Physical activity for preteens and teenagers. *Raisingchildren.net.au.* Available at: https://raisingchildren.net.au/teens/healthy-lifestyle/physical-activity/physical-activity-teens, retrieved 21 January 2020.

Centers for Disease Control and Prevention (CDC). (2020). How much physical activity do children need? *Centers for Disease Control and Prevention.* Available at: https://www.cdc.gov/physicalactivity/basics/children/index.htm, retrieved 21 January 2020.

Gilbert, M. B. (2013). A plea for systemic change in education. *On the Horizon, 21*(4): 312–22.

Gilbert, M. B. (2014). Different strokes for different folks: Connecting with students for academic success. *International Journal of Education, 6*(4): 119–31, https://doi:10.5296/ije.v6i4.6269.

Gilbert, M. B. (2018). Student performance is linked to connecting effectively with teachers. *Journal of Research of Innovation in Teaching and Learning, 12*(3): 311–24, https://doi.org/10.1108/JRIT-05-2018-0010.

Grose, J. (2020, January 8). Teach your kids to fail. *New York Times*. Available
    at: https://www.nytimes.com/2020/01/08/parenting/teach-your-kids-to-fail.
    html?searchResultPosition=1, retrieved 21 January 2020.

Haimovitz, K., & Dweck, C. S. (2016.) What predicts children's fixed and
    growth mindsets? Not their parents' views of intelligence, but the parents'
    views of failure. *Psychological Science, 271*(6): 859–69, https://doi: 10.1177/
    0956797616639727.

Nobel Coaching. (2017, May 12). Four social/emotional skills you can easily
    practice with teens. *Nobelcoaching.com*. Available at: https://nobelcoaching
    .com/emotional-skills/, retrieved 21 January 2020.

Sole-Smith, V. (2020, February 19). Your kids don't have to inherit your
    body-image issues. *New York Times*. Available at: https://parenting.nytimes
    .com/feeding/body-image-kids, retrieved 20 February 2020.

Part V

STEEP DROP

9

Sex and the Adolescent

My mother taught me ABOUT SEX:
"How do you think you got here?"

My mother taught me about GENETICS:
"You are just like your father!"

Gregory Osborn, without further attribution

HELPING WITH DECISIONS

One of the most potentially frightening occurrences in the life of adolescents is confronting their own sexuality. The onset of menstruation and the more frequent erections and nocturnal emissions are very confusing and scary.

As much as we, as parents, try to prepare our children for this hormonal upset, emerging sexuality is difficult to comprehend. Of course, there are some parents who want to avoid the situation or discussion, or pass it along to someone else.

Much of the problem stems from our own experience as sexual beings. Our own adolescence provides the model for our responses.

If we had traumatic or embarrassing encounters, it is likely that we will be ill prepared and less willing to be open and frank with our own youngsters. If we had healthy and satisfying interactions as youngsters, we will be better resources for the questions they may ask.

Another part of the problem is adolescents do not readily seek out their parents or other adults when confronted with physically private issues. They wonder in ignorance what is happening, or, even worse, they ask their friends. The amount of available *misinformation* is staggering: "You can get pregnant from a toilet set," "You can't get a girl pregnant if you pull out," etc.

Hormones run rampant in adolescents. The imbalance creates havoc with their physical, emotional, and social beings. They are usually clumsy and embarrassed when they are in sexual situations. They are either uninformed or misinformed, and mostly inexperienced.

Parents are not prepared for the inevitable, "Where did I come from?" And they are even less prepared for, "How do you do it?" (Adolescents seldom ask their parents this question, and parents usually do not initiate discussions about how to be intimate with others.) Youngsters have a difficult time imagining their parents as sexual and do not see them as having useful information to help them with their confusion.

Schools have attempted to deal with the information gap by providing programs of sex education. However, this may be a sensitive and uncomfortable topic for some parents.

Many schools address sex as part of the health curriculum. Much of what is addressed deals with the biology of conception and sexually transmitted diseases, and how to prevent both. What is sorely lacking is how people bond emotionally as an entrée to sexual relationships.

Issues of contraception and pregnancy termination are emotionally and politically charged. Schools should develop guidelines that conform to the law and community standards.

Some programs deal with, "It's okay to say no!" in response to peer pressure to engage in sex. But many programs think it is inappropriate to talk about the act of sexual intercourse and what it means to a relationship.

Adolescents are not well informed about their bodies. They are not encouraged to explore them and learn about the areas of potential intimacy. Old adages like, "If you don't stop, you'll go blind" abound. Masturbation is a normal exploratory and self-satisfying sexual experience. It cannot be prevented any more than can any other natural function. (Of course, there are some who would call anything but procreative sex unnatural.)

YOU CANNOT PREVENT SEX IN ADOLESCENTS

The *choice* to engage in sexual activity lies with the youngster, exclusively. Parents and educators can inform, but they cannot control.

More than one-third of adolescents have lost their virginity by age 16—they have "had sex." By the time they reach 20, another one-third will have had sexual intercourse.

The old guideline of waiting until marriage is no longer commonplace. This is not to say that parents should encourage their youngsters to be active sexually, only to acknowledge that they may be. On the other side of the issue is a growing number of youngsters who are choosing celibacy (and virginity) until marriage of their own accord.

The real problem is not that youngsters engage in sexual activities, but that they may not be prepared for the emotional and physical entanglements that accompany sex. If they have had no positive models, then sex will be scary and embarrassing. Being *macho* or *virginal* may not deal with the fright or assertive denial in healthy ways.

Important aspects concerning sex are learning to wait for the appropriate time in one's life to begin to have sexual relations, how to deal assertively with partners to allow sexual experiences to be positive, and, of course, to know about how to prevent conception and avoid sexually transmitted diseases. Adolescents can initiate these conversations, but oftentimes parents must be courageous to open the door for discussion. The likelihood is that they will turn to colleagues, who may be as inexperienced and misinformed as they are.

SEXUAL IDENTITY

More and more, we are confronted, either vicariously or actually, with questions and issues of sexual identity. It is confusing—for us and our children.

We tend to define our children as do those who hand them to us after birth. "Congratulations! You have a son or a daughter." It is unlikely we hear, "You have a baby, but I don't know what it is."

Sexual/gender identity may be more than obvious physical characteristics. Occasionally, there is a mismatch between the physical and the emotional. We now recognize LGBTQ—lesbian, gay, bisexual, transsexual, queer/questioning. There are other designations—pansexual, asexual, and so on (cf. Healthwise, 2018).

Some of these designations come from dysmorphia—simply described as, "I may look like a boy, but I really am a girl," or vice versa. Others may be attributed to psychosexual sources.

We have gone from sexual *preference* to sexual *orientation*. The roles and descriptions of people have expanded. Adapting to the possibilities is confusing no matter whether you are a parent or an individual trying to establish an identity.

This is a topic for parents to confront. The other is sexual relations. They arise in preteen and teen years. Both require understanding and explanation.

HAVE "THE TALK"

Many parents will avoid discussing sex for the following reasons:

They don't know how to begin.

They think it will encourage their child to have sex.

They may presume they do not know enough or that their child knows more.

The conversation can begin with questions from the youngster, but be sure you understand what the child is asking.

A humorous anecdote: A pubescent lad encountered his father one day and asked, "Dad, where did I come from?"

Not ready for the conversation, the father stumbled and bumbled about the birds and the bees and other things he thought he should say.

The son listened patiently, then replied, "Yeah, I know about that. Jimmy comes from Detroit. Where did I come from?"

See chapter 12, "Listening to Your Adolescent," and review understanding. Be sure you are answering the question that is asked.

Getting Started

Parents may avoid talking about sex or be uncertain about when to start the discussion. There is no one right answer or magical moment. Suggestions for breaking the ice are as follows:

Seize the moment. When a TV program or music video raises issues about responsible sexual behavior, use it as a springboard for discussion. Everyday moments—for example, riding in the car or putting away groceries—sometimes offer the best opportunities to talk.

Be honest. If you're uncomfortable, say so—but explain that it's important to keep talking. If you don't know how to answer your teen's questions, offer to find the answers or look them up together.

Be direct. Clearly state your feelings about specific issues, for instance, oral sex and intercourse. Present the risks objectively, including emotional pain, sexually transmitted infections, and unplanned pregnancy. For example, explain that oral sex isn't a risk-free alternative to intercourse.

Consider your teen's point of view. Don't lecture your teen or rely on scare tactics to discourage sexual activity. Instead, listen carefully. Understand your teen's pressures, challenges, and concerns.

Move beyond the facts. Your teen needs accurate information about sex—but it's just as important to talk about feelings, attitudes, and values. Examine questions of ethics and responsibility in the context of your personal or religious beliefs.

Invite more discussion. Let your teen know that it's okay to talk with you about sex whenever he or she has questions or concerns. Reward questions by saying, "I'm glad you came to me." (Mayo Clinic, 2017)

Guidelines for "the Talk"

Unless you are trained in sex education or therapy, remember that you may not be an expert. Be a source of information, but, more importantly, ask good questions.

Don't overload. If you start the conversation, talk about why the bodily changes are happening. It is usual that fathers talk with sons and mothers talk with daughters. But that is not a rule. The reverse is also appropriate.

Encourage two-way conversations.

Don't postpone until after they have become sexually active (and may be sexually awkward).

Don't overdramatize. Sex is a normal activity but has a delicate emotional component. It can be scary, exciting, and fulfilling, but it is something your child has not experienced.

Talk frankly about unprotected sex, pregnancy (with boys, too), and sexually transmitted diseases (STDs).

Address the issue of sexual pressure. "It's okay to say no." Being ready physically and being ready emotionally may be years apart.

Typical responses may be as follows: "Ewww, mom!" or "Dad, please don't . . . not again." Do not let your kids' teen angst about tough talks with mom or dad deter you (Villanueva, 2016).

The American Academy of Pediatrics (2009) has some suggestions about how youngsters can respond to the "hook" of pressure to have sex. While these seem geared toward possible responses for girls, boys, too, should not engage in sexual relations until they are ready.

There is no magic age. In addition to the emotional upheaval, parents should prepare their children to be safe, physically and emotionally. Being caught up in the heat of the moment can blur the necessary caution. Address the tough topics straightforwardly.

How will I know if I'm ready for sex? Remind your child there is no rush.

What if my boyfriend or girlfriend wants to have sex but I don't? It's okay to say no. Having sex should not be triggered by obligation or fear. Encourage your child to talk with the partner honestly.

What if I think I'm gay? Exploring feelings and questions is natural. Feelings can change. Attraction may be more about common interests than sex. Reassure your child that your love is unconditional. If it isn't, you may want to explore any fear or reservations you may have with a counselor. (Mayo Clinic, 2017)

EDUCATIONAL CONSIDERATIONS

In addition to the cognitive changes adolescent students undergo, the remarkable physical, emotional, and social changes may impinge on their education. Thoughts about the opposite sex may override focus on academics.

Issues regarding gender identity and sexual orientation can be very traumatic and upsetting. Be prepared to involve those who may have more expertise than you.

Keeping your students on track and on task can be challenging. The curriculum may not be distracting enough to keep their minds from wandering. Activities to encourage involvement in learning are crucial.

Survival Tips

- Adolescents become sexual beings.
- You cannot prevent their maturation.
- You cannot control their sexual behavior, even though you might want to.
- Prepare them for their physical and emotional changes.
- Talk with them about readiness and consequences.
- Take a breath: This is a normal stage to becoming an adult.

REFERENCES

American Academy of Pediatrics. (2009, November 2). Helping teens resist sexual pressure. *Healthychildren.org.* Available at: https://www.healthy children.org/English/ages-stages/teen/dating-sex/Pages/Helping-Teens -Resist-Sexual-Pressure.aspx, retrieved 14 October 2019.

Healthwise. (2018). Your teen's sexual orientation and gender identity. *Uofmhealth.org.* Available at: https://www.uofmhealth.org/health-library/ te7288, retrieved 27 November 2019.

Mayo Clinic. (2017). Sex education: Talking to your teen about sex. *Mayo Clinic.org.* Available at: https://www.mayoclinic.org/healthy-lifestyle/sexual -health/in-depth/sex-education/art-20044034, retrieved 24 October 2019.

Sternberg, L. (2011, February 14). Talking with your teen about sex. *Psychology Today.* Available at: https://www.psychologytoday.com/us/blog/ you-and-your-adolescent/201102/talking-your-teen-about-sex, retrieved 14 October 2019.

Villanueva, S. (2016, February 12). Teens and sex. *Psychology Today.* Available at: https://www.psychologytoday.com/us/blog/how-parent-teen/201602/ teens-and-sex, retrieved 14 October 2019.

10

Bullying

You experience many challenges parenting adolescents. Trying to keep up with their calorie consumption and quickly outgrown clothes is eye-opening and budget-jarring. The other main challenge is being aware of, adapting to, and redirecting new and unexpected behaviors.

As children approach adolescence, their burgeoning quest for independence can sometimes go awry. Trying to see themselves as special may lead to denigrating or abusing others, especially those who are different.

Aggressive behaviors toward others can lead to bullying. These behaviors are defined as *repeated* and/or *severe*, intended to or likely to hurt, control, or diminish others emotionally, physically, or sexually.

About eight percent of youngsters have been bullied, even before they grow into adolescence. Less than half report that abuse. (See prevent childabuse.org.)

FACE-TO-FACE BULLYING

(This discussion applies to those who would bully or be bullied.)

Youngsters grow at different rates, especially during adolescence. Physical size, observable sex characteristics (developing breasts, facial hair, deepening voices, etc.), and emotional maturity are typical areas for bullying.

The bully tends to have outstripped those who would be bullied in one or more of these areas or needs to feel superior. Having to be better than others may relate to not measuring up. It is easier to pick on the little kid who is smarter. I have heard it described as anyone who has one brain cell more to be a likely target.

This imbalance is the target of bullying. "If I can make you feel bad about yourself, I can feel good about myself." Other areas of focus are socioeconomics, race, religion, sexual orientation, and so forth.

The Centers for Disease Control and Prevention (2019) identified four types of bullying.

Verbal: Using words, statements, or insults in a negative way

    Name-calling

    Teasing

    Intimidation

    Threatening to cause harm

Physical: Any type of unwarranted physical force

    Hitting

    Kicking

    Tripping

    Other forms of physical aggression

Social: Harming others through manipulation or damage of their peer relationships

    Spreading rumors

    Leaving out individuals

    Embarrassing someone

    Ignoring someone

Damage to property: Damaging or threatening to damage an individual's personal belongings

As a parent, you can prepare your youngster for the possibility of what might happen as he changes. Since the onset of puberty is likely earlier than what you experienced, you should anticipate your child will begin to change somewhere between ages 10 and 14. (Of course, this is a general range.)

Be aware (beware?) of the onset. Be prepared to discuss what is happening (see KidsHealth, 2015; Vann, 2009). This should be a private conversation between you and your child. It might be a bit embarrassing and sensitive for you both.

The serious outcomes of being bullied are low self-esteem, anxiety, stress, depression, and even suicidal thoughts. On the other side, a substantial proportion of bullies may continue to be abusive and end up with criminal records.

The bottom line is to ensure that your child is aware of what is happening to him and prepare for what might happen outside of the home or online. He should be encouraged to ask questions as often as necessary and discuss any problems he may be having at school and elsewhere.

The other side of the issue is to prevent your child from becoming a bully or condoning bullying in others. Discussing differences may be a useful first topic.

Your adolescent has probably moved from the relatively safe and sheltered environment of the elementary school into the more chaotic arena of the middle/junior high school and then high school. There the students group themselves according to their interests and commonalities—competitive sports, academic interests, social adeptness, etc.

It is difficult for the school staff to monitor every interaction. Instances of bullying may be an opportunity to engage with teachers and administrators, even though the *student handbook* is likely to address the intolerance for bullying.

CYBERBULLYING

The overt bullying we see can be overshadowed by technology—*cyberbullying*. It is when someone "repeatedly makes fun of another person online or repeatedly picks on another person through e-mail or text message, or when someone posts something online about another person they don't like" (Hinduja & Patchin, 2019, p. 3).

Part of the problem is that many times the *cyberbully* can remain anonymous when spreading rumors or making hurtful comments. A whopping majority (95 percent) of teens in the United States are online, which creates huge opportunities for those who would bully or abuse.

Two primary challenges stand in the way of preventing cyberbullying: 1) Some people don't see any harm, and 2) fewer people are willing to take responsibility for responding to inappropriate use of technology.

Parents can take the lead with their own children. Be alert to the following signs:

Children being cyberbullied may

Unexpectedly stop using their device(s)

Appear nervous or jumpy when using their device(s)

Appear uneasy about being at school or outside

Appear to be angry, depressed, or frustrated after texting, chatting, using social media, or gaming

Become abnormally withdrawn

Avoid discussions about their activities

Children may be cyberbullying if they

Quickly switch screens or hide their device(s)

Use their device(s) at all hours of the night

Get unusually upset if they can't use their device(s)

Avoid discussions about what they are doing

Appear to be using multiple online accounts or an account not their own (Hinduja & Patchin, 2019)

In general, if a youngster acts inconsistently from his usual behavior when using his device(s), find out why. You are not prying (even though your child may accuse you of doing so). You are being a proactive parent for your child's safety and well-being.

TAKING ACTION

What can you do to prevent/intervene if your child is bullied or sees someone being bullied? The answer is very little to start. You can help him choose by suggesting or advising that he do the following:

Talk with an adult about the situation privately

Stand up to the bully *verbally*.

Walk away or accompany another student who was bullied (see U.S. Center for SafeSport, uscenterforsafesport.org).

If your youngster is unable or unwilling to deal with the situation, talk with school personnel or other authorities to get assistance. If the abuse is serious, contact the police. Do not confront the bully or his parents/guardians.

EDUCATIONAL CONSIDERATIONS

Issues of individual changes in adolescents are daunting enough for students. Having to confront bullies compounds an already difficult time in a child's life.

Bullying distracts from learning in major ways. Some adolescents will connive about picking on others who are different. Those being bullied may withdraw from peer interactions or avoid school altogether.

The school organization probably has a bullying policy. Teachers should know what it is and be prepared to confront bullying quickly and definitively. If there is an issue of personal safety, teachers should ask for help from a colleague or school administrator.

Safe schools are crucial for effective education (National Association of Secondary School Principals, 2019). Educators must be proactive in providing an environment in which all students are protected and productive.

Survival Tips

- Be aware of changes in your child's behavior.
- Be prepared to discuss any problems he is having, and encourage him to do likewise.
- Monitor his technology use.
- Contact appropriate authorities if your child is bullied, in person or online.
- Safe schools are mandatory.

REFERENCES

Centers for Disease Control and Prevention. (2019). Disability and safety: Information about bullying. *CDC.gov.* Available at: https://www.cdc.gov/ncbddd/disabilityandsafety/bullying.html, retrieved 11 October 2019.

Hinduja, S., & Patchin, J. W. (2019). *Cyberbullying: Identification, prevention, and response. Cyberbullying Research Center.* Available at: https://cyberbullying.org/Cyberbullying-Identification-Prevention-Response-2019.pdf, retrieved 11 October 2019.

KidsHealth. (2015). Talking with your child about puberty. *Kidshealth.org.* Available at: https://kidshealth.org/en/parents/talk-about-puberty.html, retrieved 11 October 2019.

National Association of Secondary School Principals. (2019). Safe schools. *NASSP.org.* Available at: https://www.nassp.org/policy-advocacy-center/nassp-position-statements/safe-schools, retrieved 24 October 2019.

U.S. Center for SafeSport. (2019). Available at: https://uscenterforsafesport.org, retrieved 11 October 2019.

Vann, M. R. (2009). Talking with your child about puberty. *Everyday Health, Inc.* Available at: https://www.everydayhealth.com/kids-health/talking-about-puberty.aspx, retrieved 11 October 2019.

Part VI

IN THE TUNNEL

11

Substance Abuse

Part of adolescence is exploring new territory, testing boundaries. Another part of adolescence is wanting to belong, to be a part of the group, to be accepted by peers.

We are all bombarded with a world of many and varied experiences. We see events being played out in the news. We have video games that simulate exciting and sometimes dangerous and fantastic realities.

As parents, we want to be sure our children are safe. Increasingly, they don't want us to hover and restrict them. The challenge is finding a balance between our own peace of mind and our teens' burgeoning desire to be in charge of their lives.

SUBSTANCES

The main substances that attract teen experimentation are tobacco products (cigarettes, vaping, etc.), alcohol, illicit drugs, prescription (not theirs) drugs (opioids, etc.), and marijuana (see Dryden-Edwards, 2019). Early adolescence seems to be when youngsters first try these substances. Some children may start earlier.

The confusion for parents is why. What did I do to encourage or not discourage my child from using/abusing various substances?

One answer is parental behavior and a double standard. If you use/ abuse various substances, it is unlikely that "Just say no" has much credence with your child.

If a predinner cocktail leads to two or three, you set the pattern for your child to model. It is difficult to justify that it is legal for you to use alcohol and tell your child they will have to wait until they are *of age*. What you have said is true, but it may encourage their experimentation.

Things that contribute to substance abuse in youngsters include the following:

Lack of family closeness

Frequent and unresolved conflict in the home

Parental disconnect that may lead to divorce or single parenting

Inadequate role modeling

Hypocritical morality (double standard, denial of self-destructive parental behavior)

Psychological crutches in coping with life

Communication inadequacy or gap

Religiosity

Peer pressure (cf. Rice & Dolgin, 2008)

AVOIDING DANGEROUS BEHAVIORS

Experimentation may lead to abuse or addiction. Even healthy individuals can overuse or abuse.

Examining your own behavior is a start to setting a positive example for your teen. Even if there may be no harm in a drink before dinner, in your mind, be prepared to explain why to your child.

We want our children to be safe. Most importantly, we cannot assume they will understand or embrace safe behavior if we do not talk with them.

Note: There is a difference between setting reasonable boundaries and preaching to our children. They already push back at limit setting. They want to make their own decisions. Reading them the "riot act" or saying, "Don't ever let me catch you . . ." is usually met with a mindset of "You can't tell me what to do." Have a conversation, and the younger in the lives of your children the more it is likely to take hold.

WHAT TO LOOK FOR

The preteen and early adolescent years are when youngsters may experiment. They may take the first puff of a friend's cigarette, cough, and think, "This is terrible."

They may be at a loosely supervised party and take a taste of alcohol. It will burn and not be very pleasant.

It both cases they may succumb to peer pressure and take another puff or another sip. Not wanting to seem like a nerd or uncool, they may continue to smoke or drink. (Tobacco presents the issue of physical addiction.)

Getting high may feel strange but good. The next step might be, "If I feel good now, will I feel better with more?" or "If I feel good with this, what about that?" And "that" might evolve into marijuana or illicit drugs.

Of course, all of the experiments will be done outside of the parents' view. So what do you look for?

Shifty behavior: Insisting that their room is off limits to you, sneaking out, or missing curfew

Changing relationships: Forming a new circle of friends very different from those they have had

Behavioral changes: Spewing "attitude," slamming doors, and developing a short fuse—indicators of a growing independence but can also signal more pernicious problems

Changes in school performance: A decline in grades and possible calls from school indicating concern

Changes in health: Increased illness, lethargy, crankiness, sensitivity to sunlight (Holder, 2018)

WHAT TO DO

Be careful not to attribute behavioral warning signs only to growing adolescence. If you are worried, dig deeper. Your parental instincts are not to be ignored.

As with sexual issues, which may seem tame now, have a discussion with your youngster. Try to pick a time when there has not been an explosion.

To start, reassure your child that you love and understand them but that you are concerned about the changes you are seeing. Ask about new friends and what they share.

As much as possible, let them know that you are not trying to intrude but that you are interested in what is going on in their lives. If their behavior is very worrisome, have a heart-to-heart talk about what may be causing the changes you see. Let them talk.

Don't overquestion, but do not be satisfied with limited responses. Let them know they have been heard and they can depend on you for support and guidance.

"Where did you go?"
"Out."
"What did you do?"
"Nuthin'."

Emphasize your steadfast desire to help when necessary. Be assertive about what you are prepared to do if they are not able to handle the situation themselves (consequences, counseling etc.). Do not back off just because your child gets belligerent or pushes back.

This may be one of the most dangerous roller-coaster rides you experience. It is steeper, curvier, and more dangerous than most of the others.

EDUCATIONAL CONSIDERATIONS
More and more, teachers and other educational personnel confront issues of substance abuse in students. The first part of the issue is knowing it exists. More than 90 percent of teens have started using tobacco, alcohol, and drugs.

If they have not done so already, schools need to provide training for all staff to recognize when students are "under the influence." Depending on the substance, some outward signs of use include slurred speech, dilated pupils, inappropriate laughing, stumbling, or difficulty walking.

Longer-term behaviors are as follows:

Social withdrawal

Changes in circle of friends

Personality changes

Decline in school performance

Getting sick more often (Holder, 2018)

Educators are *in loco parentis* (in place of the parent). They have an obligation to recognize and attend to changing behaviors and other warning signs.

I conducted an evaluation of a substance abuse program provided by a community agency. One of the school districts involved refused to let their students take a nationally renowned questionnaire about use of tobacco and alcohol because they thought it would encourage them to use (Gilbert, 1993).

Sticking your head in the sand will not change behavior. It will only keep it out of your sight.

Survival Tips

- Be alert to the possibility of experimentation.
- Examine your own substance use/abuse.
- Know what to look for.
- Assert your loving concerns and actions.
- Hold on tight!

REFERENCES

Dryden-Edwards, R. (2019). Teen drug abuse. *Medicinenet.com.* Available at: https://www.medicinenet.com/teen_drug_abuse/article.htm#teen_drug_abuse_facts, retrieved 15 November 2019.

Gilbert, M. B. (1993). The use of cognitive and affective measures to evaluate early intervention alcohol/drug education programs. *Journal of Alcohol and Drug Education, 38*(3): 89–104. (ERIC Document Accession No. EJ468335)

Holder, A. (2018). Five warning signs of teen drug and alcohol abuse. *Safelandingrecovery.com.* Available at: https://www.safelandingrecovery.com/post/5-warning-signs-of-teen-drug-and-alcohol-abuse, retrieved 27 November 2019.

Rice, F. P., & Dolgin, K. G. (2008). *The adolescent: Development, relationships, and culture* (12th ed.). Upper Saddle River, NJ: Pearson.

Part VII

INTO THE DAYLIGHT

12

Listening to Your Adolescent

"Mary, it's bedtime."

"Mary, it's 9:30. Please turn off the TV and go to bed."

"MARY LOUISE BROWN, if you don't turn off the TV this instant . . ."

This script plays out innumerable times as parents interact with their children. What parents may not recognize is that children have them well trained. That is, a child will not do what she does not want to do until her parents reach their breaking point—usually after the request has been made three times. At the third request—by now a parental mandate issued in a slow, deliberate, and very loud voice—the youngster understands she will have to do what the exasperated parent demands.

The other side of this issue can be the poor listening model the parent has been for the child. Of all of the communication skills, listening is the one we do the poorest. Perhaps, it is because we had poor listening models and were not taught how to listen. The end result is we do not listen well—to our children and, probably, to others.

Parents are the leaders of the family—having a goal or vision of the future and encouraging family members to move toward that vision. But leading the family "is not for the timid. It requires listening to family members and confronting inappropriate and unacceptable behavior. That is, one has to love family members enough to confront them and then allow them to suffer the natural consequences of their actions" (Steil & Bommelje, 2004, p. 23).

Children receive little of our attention when we do not engage them for several reasons. We may ignore them or not try to understand fully what they want. Why?

1. We are preoccupied and do not pay attention.
2. We make up our minds in advance, waiting to say "no."
3. We are angry with the child.
4. We let words upset us.
5. We think the story or explanation is too long.
6. We listen for bits and pieces of information.
7. We jump to conclusions.
8. We interrupt.
9. We engage in selective perception.
10. We misunderstand because words have different meanings for different people. (Lyle, 1984)

It may be inconvenient for us to set aside our schedule when our children want our attention. We tend to *postpone* them. So it is not surprising they do not pay attention when *we* speak to them.

One of the most poignant stories was told to me by a man who described his typical arrival at home in the evening. His wife was preparing supper and trying to tell him of her day; the television was blaring; the children wanted his attention; and all he wanted to do was unwind and read the newspaper.

After we had talked about how to listen more effectively, he shared that between the initial and follow-up sessions, he had changed his listening behavior at home. One evening when his son wanted to tell his father what he had done during the day, the man took him into a room with no distractions, and, according to the father, for 30 minutes they had the most meaningful interchange in all of the eight years they had had together.

What the man had done was not magical or difficult. He had given undivided attention to his son in an atmosphere free from distractions—internal or external. The power of this attention may be obvious. The child became an important part of his father's life.

Early attempts at effective listening can only help the connection you have with your youngster, so when difficulties arise, either for the youngster (for example, going through puberty into adolescence) or in the family, a strong relationship has been established to confront these difficulties.

"Humans listen before they speak, speak before they read, and read before they write. Thus, failure to refine our listening skills impairs the entire process of human communication" (Wolff, & Marsnik, 1993).

It is important to understand that communication is not simply having two people talking to (at?) one another, waiting for their turn to speak. Communication happens when one person understands a message in the same way the other intended it to be understood (Johnson, 1993).

If you listen *actively*, you can establish closer relationships and make communication events more effective. This means making eye contact, using supportive facial expressions, asking questions to confirm or clarify what you have understood, and responding appropriately (Zimmerman, 1986).

HOW TO LISTEN BETTER

In most families, the question of who is in charge, or who has the *power*, is constant. Parents want to be in control; children test the limits of what can be controlled.

When the limits are reasonable (in the minds of the parents) and the children stay within them, peace exists. When children exceed the limits, a battle can occur. (We have gotten on the roller coaster, again.)

The first response of a parent to a breach is to demand that the child behave *properly*. Look at Mary's behavior (at the beginning of the chapter). She wants to watch TV past her normal bedtime. Her parent demands she *follow the rules*. She may comply with her parent's demands, but she will do so grudgingly.

Why does she want to stay up later? Just to be obstinate or disobedient? Possibly. Or might it be that she is engaged in something on TV that is important to her? Whatever the reason, her parent has not listened to her.

Staying up (too) late has its consequences (Dreikurs & Grey, 1990). The natural one is that the child may be tired the next day. (We know youngsters need at least eight to nine hours of sleep a night. Adolescents may need more.) The logical consequence is parents usually punish a child who "breaks the rules."

Think about this alternative: Ask the child why she wants to watch TV past her usual bedtime. *Listen* carefully to her answer, then reflect your understanding of what she said. If the answer is reasonable, you may decide to *bend* the rules—as an exception, which should be clear.

So how do we listen—or listen better? Here are some suggestions:

Find areas of common interest. Ask, "What's in this for me?" What is your child trying to communicate, and how are you involved?

Judge content, not delivery. Concentrate on the main message. Is what your child is asking reasonable?

Hold your fire. Withhold judgment until the message is complete. Let your child finish her thought. Do not interrupt, even though you may have a particular position. Be sure you understand the message.

Be flexible. Consider carefully whether your position is the right one, not just the one you have always used. For example, as the child gets older, it is okay to change bedtime. Is now that time for Mary?

Work at listening. Make eye contact, and support the conversation with open facial expressions; ask questions to be sure you understand; and respond appropriately.

Resist distractions. Fight or avoid distractions: Put aside the things that you are thinking (and recognize when your concentration is waning or absent).

Keep your mind open. Know your emotional triggers and be prepared to combat their control of you. These are the words, phrases, or vocal tones that you find objectionable. A child's challenge may be enough to set us off: "How dare you talk to me that way?" Sometimes, children are not polite or considerate. If the situation is emotional, it may not be the best time to teach manners. Save that lesson for a less stressful time. (This is hard for some people. They feel their parental "power" is in jeopardy and that they need to maintain their control of their children.)

Capitalize on the fact that you can think (two to three times) faster than others can speak. Use the spare mental time to anticipate, summarize, and reflect on what has been said; weigh the evidence; listen between the lines. (Nichols & Stevens, 1957; Faber & Mazlish, 2005; Steil, Barker, & Watson, 1983)

COMMUNICATING BETTER

Listening well is just one part of communicating. We have to *understand* what the child wants us to understand to complete the "loop" (Johnson, 1993).

We have to *accept* the feelings of our child, along with understanding the words (Bolton, 1986; Faber & Mazlish, 2005). If we go to, "You really don't feel like that" or "That's a terrible way to feel," we invite the child to push us away, be confused, or become defensive.

With Mary (mentioned earlier), we might offer, "I understand the television program is important to you." This opens the door to a discussion. (Of course, recording the program may also be an option.)

In adolescence, teenagers tend to rebel against authority. They test the limits of what they can do. They resent being told what to do or how to think. They comply less and resist more.

One thought is to involve them in decisions that affect them (recall chapter 5). This involvement can be at several levels:

Participating (getting input) in providing information. The parent still makes the final decision (for instance, where the family may go for dinner or on vacation).

Joining (making decisions together). Whatever the *group* decides is what will be done. The parent participates and supports the final decision.

Independence (no active involvement by parent). The parent turns over the decision to the youngster and supports what she decides.

One word of caution: You must decide what level of involvement is comfortable to you. If you are not ready to allow your youngster to make her own decisions, avoid independence until you are ready (but don't wait too long or be unreasonable). Trust can be damaged if you tell your teenager she can make the decision and then veto it.

Going back to Mary, we might start with, "Mary, your usual bedtime is 9:30. Is there something special you are watching?" (This is a statement of established behavior followed with a request for information.) If her response is reasonable, you might say, "I think it will be okay for you to watch this, but off to bed after it is over. Okay?" (Wait for compliant acknowledgment of your question.)

You have done several things here: You have become flexible, shown Mary she has some input, and also established a pattern for the future.

If you feel it necessary, you might emphasize, "This is only for tonight. You know how you feel when you do not get enough sleep." (This should be posed as a reminder, not a warning.)

Teenagers tend to remember changes in patterns. Later, you may hear, "Well, you let me stay up late before." Be prepared for another discussion or a continuing battle concerning an issue until the changes are permanent. (Avoid the roller coaster! You may get emotional whiplash.)

Another part of listening well, or communicating, is reflecting accurate understanding of the message you have received. One technique is "Reflecting to yes" (Fisher, Ury, & Patton, 2011). Until you get an unqualified "Yes" from your youngster in response to your understanding, you have not understood the message fully.

"You want to stay up later to watch TV."

"Yes, but this is an important show."

"Oh, you want to watch this program."

"Yes. I will go to bed as soon as it's over."

Two things here: First, "Yes, but . . ." indicates your incomplete understanding. You have to go further. Second, your response should be *stated* simply. It is not a question or a request for more information.

Listening effectively is the first step in successful interactions with your adolescent. The next chapter will go deeper into how to communicate well.

To connect with your adolescent, do the following:

Be authentic. Show that you care about what your teen has to say.

Be visible. Chat face-to-face whenever possible.

Listen carefully. Reflect your understanding of the message, *before* you offer counterpoints or advice (Leading Effectively Staff, 2018). Wait until she is finished.

EDUCATIONAL CONSIDERATIONS

(Listening has been increasingly recognized as a crucial skill. Some standardized tests have added a listening component, but a mandate for listening instruction in schools has not been realized [see Gilbert, 1986, 1988, 1999].)

Engagement is a crucial concept for learning to occur. It means more than only one person talking at a time.

Students can obey the classroom rules of raising their hand and waiting to be recognized before chiming in. However, this does not indicate they are listening. Many times, when a hand is raised, the listening mechanism is turned off. The student is waiting for a turn to talk, forming her contribution. Or they just may be quiet, or daydreaming, or fantasizing about other things.

Another aspect of poor listening in the classroom is having to repeat instructions (remember Mary?). If you, as a teacher, find yourself having to repeat yourself, redefine your expectations and behavior. Tell your students you will say things only once. It is their responsibility to attend.

Resist repeating instructions: "What did you say the assignment was?" Rather than responding directly, offer, "If you need more information, check with a friend."

You have to change your behavior if you expect students to change theirs. How much time is wasted on repetition for no reason other than students were not paying attention?

However, you have to decide how you will get the students' attention. Your speaking may not be enough.

Of course, you can write instructions on the board or in a handout (physical or electronic). You must find something that captures the moment.

"Class, I have tomorrow's assignment for you." Then wait for signs of attention—eye contact, alert body posture, etc. You may also want to ask one of the students to indicate her understanding of the information by repeating it out loud.

If you want students to listen (attend) better, you have to create an environment where listening is important. Setting an example of good listening yourself is a way to start.

If what you are saying is important, wait for attention. Prompt silence (gently) if necessary. Multiple messages (e.g., people talking about different things) invites confusion and selective listening.

An ancillary lesson to encourage better listening may be accomplished in three activities:

1. Ask students to get a partner. Then ask all of them to think of a message. (Content is unimportant.) When you say "Go" or "Start," each partner is to deliver the message simultaneously. (Do not let this noisy confusion go for more than 30 seconds or so.) Ask the students if they understood what their partner was saying. If each of them was talking, the answer should be, "No." This is the "party." It seems that everyone is talking, and no one is listening.

2. Again with a partner, ask each student to think of a message. When you indicate they should start, one will begin. The other is not to talk until the first person pauses, stops, and takes a breath. Then the second person delivers his or her message. This is called "conflicting agenda," two people delivering unrelated messages.

3. With a partner, one person delivers a message. The other person cannot begin until he or she has reflected understanding of the message until the original sender agrees by word or gesture that communication has occurred—understanding to the sender's satisfaction. Then the roles are reversed. This is "active listening."

Ask the students which activity worked best for communication. You will probably get affirmation that active listening worked best (even though the other activities may be fun.)

Survival Tips

- Effective listening means understanding what your child wants you to understand.
- Listening is a skill that takes practice.
- Be sure that your child understands what you want her to understand by getting a compliant "Yes."
- Listening is the first step to communicating well.
- Be an example of good listening.

REFERENCES

Bolton, R. G. (1986). *People skills: How to assert yourself, listen to others, and resolve conflicts.* New York: Simon & Schuster.

Dreikurs, R., & Grey, L. (1990). *Logical consequences: A new approach to discipline.* New York: Dutton.

Faber, A., & Mazlish, E. (2005). *How to talk so teens will listen and listen so teens will talk.* New York: HarperCollins.

Fisher, R., Ury, W. L., & Patton, B. (2011). *Getting to yes: Negotiating agreement without giving in* (3rd ed.). New York: Penguin.

Gilbert, M. B. (1986). Do principals listen? *NFEAS Journal, 3*(3): 115–20.

Gilbert, M. B. (1988). Listening at work: Work at listening. *Shaping the Future, 1*(1): 22–31.

Gilbert, M. B. (1999). Why educators have problems with some students: Understanding frames of preference. *Journal of Educational Administration, 37*(3): 243–55. (ERIC Document Accession No. EJ592943)

Johnson, D. (1993). *Reaching out: Interpersonal effectiveness and self-actualization* (5th ed.). Englewood Cliffs, NJ: Prentice-Hall.

Leading Effectively Staff. (2018, March 14). Why communication is so important for leaders. *Center for Creative Leadership.* Available at: https://

www.ccl.org/articles/leading-effectively-articles/communication-1-idea-3
-facts-5-tips/, retrieved 17 January 2020.

Lyle, M. (1984, March). *Teaching listening skills for parents.* Presentation at
the fifth annual convention of the International Listening Association,
Scottsdale, Arizona.

Nichols, R. G., & Stevens, L. A. (1957). *Are you listening?* New York:
McGraw-Hill.

Steil, L. K., Barker, L. L., & Watson, K. W. (1983). *Effective listening: Key to
your success.* Reading, MA: Addison-Wesley.

Steil, L. K., & Bommelje, R. K. (2004). *Listening leaders: The ten golden rules to
listen, lead, and success.* Edina, MN: Beaver Pond Press.

Wolff, F. I., & Marsnik, N. (1993). *Perceptive listening* (2nd ed.). Fort Worth,
TX: Harcourt.

Zimmerman, A. (1987). *Effective listening strategies.* Presentation at the eighth
annual convention of the International Listening Association, New Orleans,
Louisiana.

13

Communicating with Your Adolescent

CLONING IS UNLIKELY

We have spawned, sired, bred, procreated. Most of us have a genetic link with our children. We have mixed our genetic information to create the wonderful beings that are our children. But they are different.

We expect they will be like us—physically and, especially, behaviorally. These expectations are not unreasonable—until we realize that our children may see the world differently and seem to have *strange* needs and desires.

"How can you listen to that noise?"

"Huh?"

"That music, if that's what you call it, is horrible!"

"Wha'd ya mean?"

Even if we adopt or foster-parent adolescents, we must recognize that the changing individuals are unique. They see the world differently than we do.

What we have begun to experience can be described in illuminating detail (Kahler, 1982; Pauley, Bradley, & Pauley, 2001; Gilbert, 2012). Each of us has a personality structure much like a six-story condominium, with a "ground floor" and higher "floors" in a particular sequence for ourselves. (There are 720 possible variations.) This is a structure we own and owe no money on, requiring little or no maintenance. (Of course, regular "housekeeping" is required—keeping things neat and tidy.)

The condo represents who we are. It might look like this.

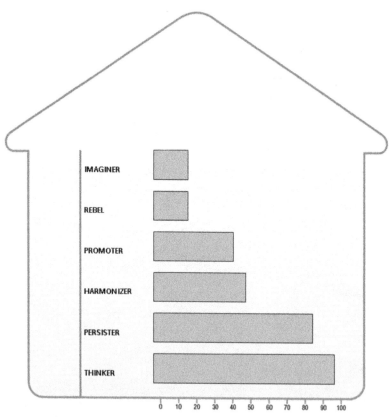

FIGURE 13.1
Sample Personality Condominium

Figure 13.1 shows the six floors that make up this person. His strongest (most well *furnished*) floor is his Thinker. In fact, this floor is so well furnished he could not get another knickknack to fit.

A person could spend all day on this floor, interacting with others. The only reason to go elsewhere is because of an invitation from someone or an issue that suggests one might access another floor.

Next to the floor is the elevator that allows him to travel to the other floors. Each higher floor may not have as much furnishing as the one beneath it. Some other things can still be added. Some expansion can occur.

In this case, the *second* floor seems to be full. He has spent enough time there to complete the furnishing.

If we look carefully, we see that the top floor has very little. If we continue to think of furnishings, it is not very inviting.

That is how we, as people, are. We each have six personality floors, with varying degrees of furnishing (*energy*).

Each personality floor is furnished in a way that describes different strengths, how we prefer to see the world, what we need to motivate us, and what happens, *predictably*, when we do not get what we need. Positively, we want to get our needs met to be able to move through our world in energetic and productive ways.

On the negative side, when we do not get our needs met, we move into distress and, even without our awareness, attempt to get our needs met negatively. These distress sequences are the basis for the conflicts we experience, for example, trying to get our children to embrace our values.

As parents, we cannot imagine why our children act differently than we would or than we encourage or demand. One answer is that they are different, and how they see things and what they need are not the same as what we see and need.

We see three predominant personality strengths in most parents—the Harmonizer, the Thinker, and the Persister. The *Harmonizer* type within us is *compassionate, sensitive,* and *warm*. She wants people, especially those close to her, to be okay. (Seventy-five percent of the North American population [all data are from Kahler, 1982], having Harmonizer as the strongest part, is female.) She needs to be *accepted for herself* and sees her world through her *feelings and senses*. She will try to *fix* things or people when they are out of order—sometimes putting her own needs aside.

The *Thinker* type within us is *logical, responsible,* and *organized*. He (75 percent of Thinkers are male) wants *structure* in his life. People are OK if they think clearly and are *on time*. He needs *recognition for his work* and sees his world through thoughts and ideas. He will become fussy and grumpy about what is fair and attempts to overcontrol others when he does not get what he needs (is in distress).

The *Persister* type within us is *conscientious, observant,* and *dedicated*. He (75 percent of Persisters are male) has *strong beliefs*. People are OK if they are committed (to a belief, value, or cause). He needs to have others *accept his convictions* and acknowledge that he is doing something important. He will begin to crusade about what he believes is important when he is distressed.

These three personality types make up about two-thirds of the North American population (who have been profiled using Kahler's [1999] *Personality Pattern Inventory*). They communicate especially well with others who have similar needs and see the world in similar ways. They may have (great) difficulty with others who need different things and see the world differently.

Two personality types within all of us that can cause problems for the first three are Rebels and Promoters. They are very outgoing.

We see a lot of Rebel behaviors in adolescents. However, this does not mean all adolescents are strongest in these personality types. They are going through an *evolution* and can mimic rebellious behavior.

The *Rebels* within us are *spontaneous, creative,* and *playful*. They draw their seemingly boundless energy from exciting *contact* with people and things. They need to have *fun*—even before doing other things. When they do not have fun, they will pretend to be confused and eventually blame other people and things for what is not going well. They challenge the Thinker and Persister in parents, who want them to either think right or follow the rules. These same parents will stress that one must finish one's work *before* playing. The Rebel has to get her play *batteries* charged *before* working.

The *Promoters* within us are *adaptable, persuasive,* and *charming.* They need to have a lot going on in their lives. Their energy comes from *action*—typically taken in short, tangible bursts. Taking a lot of time with projects and waiting for the future to achieve goals will be distressful to them. They will try to *rewrite* the rules, manipulate the situation to their advantage, or create situations where others will be in conflict. Promoters, too, are challenging for their parents whose preferences and needs are different.

The remaining personality type is the *Imaginer,* who is *imaginative, reflective,* and *calm.* This personality type within us needs *solitude* and usually prefers to be directed to act. Too much activity or interaction with others is distressful. This individual will begin to withdraw and become very passive when confronted with too much action. Parents who do not understand Imaginer types will question why they always have to be told to do something or why they want to be alone so much. Is there something wrong with them? No!

All of these personality types are OK. They are no more or less intelligent, nor can they be changed into something they are not. Parents who spend a great deal of time, energy, and money attempting to make their *different* children in the parent's own image will be greatly frustrated and create a difficult family situation. In such cases, adolescents will get their needs met outside of the family and, in the direst of situations, remove themselves from the family, either emotionally or physically, or both.

Since most people come to parenthood without formal preparation and often copy the models most familiar to them, their parenting cannot be expected to be successful unless their children are like them naturally. Only then will they be able to communicate effectively. (This presumes the patterns they know best are appropriate.)

BECOMING A BETTER PARENT

The lack of preparation for parenting provides challenges for us to interact with adolescents effectively. One of the first things parents must do is to see their children in a positive light, even if that light is tinted differently.

Most of us want our children to do the right things and grow up to be happy people. Those goals of being right and happy speak to who we are as parents and people. Some of us focus on rules, structure, and values; others of us feel first.

If our children share these goals, the home is not likely to be a battleground. If not, let the games begin. You will have an endless pass on the roller coaster.

As children enter adolescence, they begin to test the boundaries:

"What can I do that I have not done before?"

"Can I make more of my own decisions?"

"Won't my parents ever leave me alone?

As discussed earlier, parents do not have a rulebook to give them a schedule as to when and if to *back off*. There is no magic formula, either. Youngsters should be given decisions that are rightly theirs to make—with increasingly broader limits as they get older. If they do not practice good decision making as they mature, they will not be prepared to make good decisions when they become adults.

If you and your children are different in the way you see things and what you need to keep you energized, a number of different games may emerge. One of the favorites is, "Yes . . . but."

"I want you home by 10:00."

"Yes, but the party isn't over until 11:00. Can't I stay longer?"

"You have a hard enough time getting up as it is, and we have to be in church by 9:30 for your cousin's confirmation. We have been planning this for a long time."

"Yeah, I know, but everyone will think I'm a nerd if I go home early."

"What others think of you is not as important as what we do as a family."

"Yes, but I'll set my alarm so I'll be ready in time. Please?"

"Why don't you . . .?"

"Yes, but . . ."

And the game progresses until someone *wins*—and that someone is usually the parent, especially if she is not willing to compromise, or until the child is no longer willing to *play*—that is, he gives up or loses the will to win.

Games have no upside. Someone wins, and someone loses. There are usually no ties.

(Parents who want to dominate their children's decisions are threatened by relinquishing any power they think they have. This position may come back to haunt them later on.)

Adolescents want to make their own decisions. They want to be independent from their parents for some things. (Some might say from all things.)

They relish what their parents provide (shelter, food, clothing, etc.) but are less and less willing to comply with their parents' wishes if the wishes or rules keep them from doing what they want to do. They may not have the effective decision-making tools they need.

Finding boundaries is hard. On one hand, we want our children to do what is right and be safe. On the other hand, we want to stay connected to them.

> Because of his communication and interaction style, a youngster was having some difficulty in school. He connected well with some teachers and not with others. He was fitful in his performance—doing very well in some classes and having serious difficulty in others. (Performance and connection are related.)
>
> He was also an excellent athlete. He had the potential to go on to college and compete athletically there.
>
> Without success, his father could not get him to work better in school. He finally decided to postpone his son's athletics until his schoolwork improved. This was an extremely hard decision, and his son resented it. However, it was the incentive the youngster needed to improve.

Was this the best approach? Not necessarily. The parent made the decision for the youngster for good reasons (in the parent's mind). If pressed, the youngster might say he resented the parent's decision, even though he knew he could do better in school.

Long-term consequences are not usually uppermost in the minds of adolescents. Parents try to guide them, using their own experiences and visions for what their youngsters need. Most children live in the here and now.

Parents shepherd their children along their journey to independence, hoping the eventual destination will be positive. Sometimes the route is smooth and navigated easily. Other times they hitch a ride on the roller coaster, with its steep turns and loops.

KNOW YOURSELF FIRST

Many of us move through our lives without really knowing who we are. If someone would ask us, "Who are you?" we might respond by talking about what we have done—our jobs, families, etc. But is there more to know?

For us to communicate with people effectively, especially those who are different, we must know who we are. This means understanding how we see the world and what motivates us.

HOW TO COMMUNICATE BETTER

To communicate effectively, you must be in an OK place. If your day has not gone well, you may need some time to energize yourself if someone seeks your attention.

The first aspect of how we communicate is the primary screen through which we experience people and events. This is called *perception.*

There are six possibilities, identified by Kahler's Process Communication Model (PCM) (1982) and connected to the aforementioned personality types:

1. Emotions (Harmonizers)
2. Thoughts (Thinkers)
3. Opinions (Persisters)
4. Inactions (reflections) (Imaginers)
5. Reactions (like and dislikes) (Rebels)
6. Actions (Promoters)

Preference for one of these perceptions is observable early in one's life. It continues to predominate within individuals. None is better than any other, and they are not related to intelligence. The primary perception does not appear to be explained by genetics or environment.

(When I asked Dr. Kahler whether the base perception was caused/ formed by *nature* or *nurture*, he replied, "Yes." Even in his playfulness and later with fuller explanation, he said we do not know.)

An interesting aspect of PCM is that each has some of each of the other perceptions. They combine to construct a hierarchy describing each person (see figure 13.1).

The character strengths of each personality type are described in this chapter, along with motivational needs. When those needs are not met positively, we can predict what behavior we are likely to see.

Distress Patterns

Unfulfilled needs interrupt effective communication and interaction. These needs motivate us and put us in a position of seeing ourselves and others as okay. When we do not get our needs fulfilled positively, we move into predictable negative behaviors. The first behavior we see calls attention to the beginning of distress. Each personality type has one. If the distress continues, we put on one of three *masks*: Drooper, Attacker, or Blamer. Each mask indicates a particular unmet need. (See table 13.1.)

Table 13.1. Distress Patterns

Personality	Need	Driver	Mask Behavior
Harmonizer	Acceptance of self; sensory	Overadapting to others	Drooper: Wilting, inviting criticism
Thinker	Recognition of work; time structure	Taking on more tasks	Attacker: Fussy about responsibility, money, time
Persister	Recognition of work; conviction	Focusing on what's wrong	Attacker: Preaching, crusading
Imaginer	Solitude	Withdrawing	Drooper: Stalled
Rebel	(Playful) contact	Expecting others to think for them	Blamer: Blaming others, blameless
Promoter	Incidence	Withdrawing support	Blamer: Manipulating, getting others to argue/fight

Dealing with Distress

If we are getting our own needs met, we can try to help our adolescent in distress. If we are also in distress, we are in the loop-de-loop of the roller-coaster ride—down, up, and side to side, hoping the ride is over soon.

Interrupting distress means we have to try to get our needs met positively or help others, or both. Dealing with our own distress means we understand what we need to be OK. Dealing with our adolescent allows us to focus on what he needs. Presuming we are OK, we can attempt to help him get his needs met positively. (See table 13.2.)

Table 13.2. Distress Intervention

Personality	Need	Approach	Example
Harmonizer	Acceptance of self; sensory	Nurturing	"You are a good person."
Thinker	Recognition of work; time structure	Requesting information	"What do you think would work better?"
Persister	Recognition of work; conviction	Requesting opinion	"What do you believe is the right approach?"
Imaginer	Solitude	Directing	"Clean up your room now, please."
Rebel	(Playful) contact	Interacting playfully	"Dude, let's try this another way."
Promoter	Incidence	Directing	"Finish your chores before you leave."

Insisting our way is right usually brings on either more arguing or resentment. Yes, we can win the battle, but we have not resolved whatever the issue is. Communicating effectively with our adolescent is more time-consuming. If we interact well, we continue to build a functional and respectful relationship. (The roller-coaster rides can be saved for family vacations at a theme park.)

Owning Up and Apologizing

How do we filter our messages? Initially, we use our base perceptions (as described earlier). The other filters we may use are social. They allow others to see us positively. They

Protect the feelings of others

Save us from being embarrassed

Show respect for those in charge

Help us stay out of trouble (Kuzma, 2008)

When our social filters are either not well developed or undeveloped, we might say or do things that are hurtful to others. Sometimes we may be intentional by teasing or being indelicate: "Where did you get that ugly sweater?" Other times, we just may not know better: "That's so easy. Everyone can do it." (Here we may not understand the limitations of another person.)

Closely connected with our social filters is impulse control. Being too quick with a response without thinking carefully of its impact can be damaging to a relationship.

Teens can be cruel to one another because they do not control their impulses or do not activate whatever good social filters they have. These are learned responses that should be taught at home and in school.

One of the hardest things we have to do is apologize when we have made mistakes or misstepped. It is as difficult for adults as it is for kids.

Egos are involved. Most adolescents already have fragile egos, and denting them is something they will try to avoid.

Being a member of a group allows adolescents opportunities to apologize when they err—certainly if they want to stay in good standing in the group. With adults, siblings, and others, they resist.

To apologize takes emotional regulation—calming down and considering others' feelings. This is something the turbulence of adolescence flails against. It reveals vulnerability.

If your teen has done something egregious without owning up, for instance, denting the car, focus on how he or she will make amends. Another example would be saying something that is either mean or thoughtless. Do not insist on an empty apology. This is only heard as, "Admit you're a bad person" (Realsimple.com, 2016, p. 115). And a power struggle ensues. Crank up the roller coaster.

Teens may be as sorry they got caught as they are with the incident itself. Whether what happened is their fault or not, learning to apologize gracefully and sincerely is ego building. The momentary embarrassment will vanish and be replaced with self-affirmation.

EDUCATIONAL CONSIDERATIONS
When students reach adolescence, teachers have to confront more than just academic differences. Now the full range of changes is in full view, challenging everyone to ride the roller coaster or stay on the ground. Dealing with the social, emotional, and physical changes can offer different choices of roller coasters.

Without resilience and sufficient energy, it is easy to want to exclude "crazy" and unpredictable behavior from the classroom. This is usually not an option.

Performance varies. Students whose learning preferences are similar to the teacher's choice of instructional delivery tend to do better (Gilbert, 2014, 2018).

Assessment standards for classroom performance are usually set by the teachers. The assignment of grades is based on student ability to meet teacher expectations. Students identified as "easy to communicate with" significantly outstrip their counterparts labeled as "difficult to communicate with" (Bailey, 1998; Cicinelli, 2013; Gilbert, 2018; Wallin, 1993).

Since most teachers see the world through either their thoughts, beliefs, or emotions, those students who match up with those perceptions are more likely to achieve better than those who are different. This latter group prefers reactions (likes and dislikes), actions, or reflections as their primary filters.

When standardized (norm-referenced) tests are used to measure performance, the differences tend to reduce or disappear altogether. Teachers are the linchpins. When they are taken out of the mix, students perform more evenly. The crucial part of learning is teachers connecting with students effectively. To do that, they have to be positively motivated regularly. This means they get their preeminent needs met consistently. Without positive needs fulfillment, they are subject to the same predictable distress as the students.

Content is the focal learning measurement. Those who can demonstrate more knowledge and aptitude are the more successful. To provide a productive learning environment, the delivery *process* is crucial.

A multimodal approach is likely to connect with all students. Those who are more external in their learning preferences will respond positively to kinesthetic and tactile activities. Those who are more internal (like their teachers) will prefer visual and auditory input.

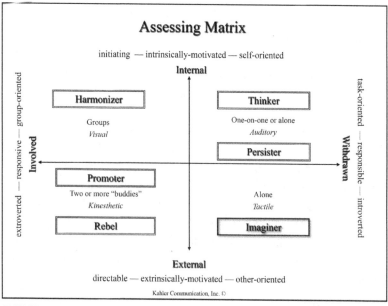

FIGURE 13.2
Assessing Matrix (adapted from Kahler, 1996, and Dr. Okie Lee Wolfe, personal communication)

The adapted Assessing Matrix (figure 13.2) shows the presumed learning styles preferred by each personality type. With teachers mostly (90 percent) intrinsically oriented, they may misconnect with those students who prefer hands-on delivery—the 35 percent who are extrinsically oriented (Rebels, Promoters, and Imaginers) (Gilbert, 1994–2018).

Every student can adapt to any type of instruction, given adequate motivation. A steady diet of something less preferred may cause learning "indigestion." This upset may lead to distressful behavior. If teachers are adept at understanding the "misbehavior," they can intervene to bring the students into a positive place. Lack of understanding, especially if teachers are in distress, can lubricate the roller coasters.

Hang on! It may be a wild ride.

Survival Tips

- Remember: "Say a kind word to someone who looks up to you in awe, because that little person soon will grow up and leave your side."—George Carlin.

- Getting needs met positively is an important part of being OK.

- Not getting needs met positively brings on predictable distress.

- Teachers are as susceptible as students to distress.

- "What is happening now is my genuine life. Like it or not, want it or not, this life is what is. To embrace it rather than push it away is the key to freedom."—Ezra Bayda

- Reinforce acceptance of making mistakes and apologizing sincerely.

- Teach the curriculum to the students, not vice versa.

REFERENCES

Bailey, R. C. (1998). *An investigation of personality types of adolescents who have been rated by classroom teachers to exhibit inattentive and/ or hyperactive impulsive behaviors.* Unpublished doctoral dissertation, University of Arkansas at Little Rock.

Cicinelli, A. (2013). *Communication styles: An examination of ability to communicate with students and student achievement in Michigan public schools.* Unpublished doctoral dissertation, Central Michigan University.

Gilbert, M. B. (1994–2018). Unpublished ongoing research.

Gilbert, M. B. (2012). *Communicating effectively* (2nd ed.). Lanham, MD: Scarecrow Education.

Gilbert, M. B. (2014). Different strokes for different folks: Connecting with students for academic success. *International Journal of Education, 6*(4): 119–31, https://doi:10.5296/ije.v6i4.6269.

Gilbert, M. B. (2018). Student performance is linked to connecting effectively with teachers. *Journal of Research in Innovative Teaching and Learning, 12*(3): 311–24, https://doi.org/10.1108/JRIT-05-2018-0010.

Kahler, T. (1982). *Process Communication Model.* Little Rock, AR: Kahler Communications.

Kahler, T. (1996). *Process Education Model.* Little Rock, AR: Kahler Communications.

Kahler, T. (1999). *Personality Pattern Inventory.* Little Rock, AR: Kahler Communications.

Kuzma, J. D. (2008, October). Our social filter. *Jillkuzma.files.wordpress.com.* Available at: https://jillkuzma.files.wordpress.com/2008/11/brain-social -filter.pdf, retrieved 13 February 2020.

Pauley, J. A., Bradley, D. F., & Pauley, J. F. (2001). *Here's how to reach me.* Baltimore, MD: Paul H. Brookes.

Realsimple.com. (2016, May). How to teach your kids to say sorry. *Real Simple,* p. 115.

Wallin, M. B. (1993). "Making" the grade: The effects of teacher personality types on student grading practices. *Dissertation Abstracts International-A, 53*(11). (University Microfilms No. AAT 9307147, Arizona State University)

Part VIII

LEVELING OFF

14

Epilogue

Okay, the roller coaster is slowing down. Nothing overly dramatic has happened. You experienced some loops and bumps, but everyone has survived.

Your adolescent is finding her equilibrium. She talks to you with respect—and even what appears to be affection and admiration. She seems ready to move on to whatever is next. She is excited about her burgeoning independence, but she may be unsure about leaving the comfort of the home she has shared with you. You are breathing more easily, but with a knot in your midsection. You wonder if you have done enough to prepare her for being away from home.

Is she a successful decision maker now? Does she know how to manage her money? Can she find her way?

HOW DO YOU FEEL?

You may feel like you have been kicked in the gut. You cannot catch your breath. You are worried beyond imagining. You may grieve for a time at the *loss* of her presence, her closeness, her physical affection.

You have done all you knew how to do. The bumps, turns, and loops are but a memory. Something, someone is missing.

If the parting is something you have anticipated and planned, the departure may be softened. If you have argued about where she is going, with whom she will live, or where she will be, it may be a harder separation.

Regardless of the reason, she is gone. Your role in her life has taken on a new dimension.

Part on the best terms possible. Cut the umbilical cord or apron strings, or just turn loose. Recognize she is still your baby, your child, but treat her as an adult. You have both earned it.

WHERE DO YOU GO FROM HERE?

Now comes the really hard part—turning loose. When your adolescent is ready to leave home—whether to go to college or just live independently, it is time for you to gather your courage and wish her well. This does not mean total disengagement. It means you recognize her as an adult, fully capable of surviving without your daily oversight.

Assure her you are just a text, electronic chat, or phone call away if she wants to talk. Also, *ask* if it is OK for you to touch base from time to time. You may need a "kid" fix to be sure she is okay.

Let her know she is always welcome, but be careful of inferring she can always come home. If it is a place where she can always go and be taken in, she is not truly independent.

You may not want her to be independent; you want to hold on. There are still vestiges of the child she was. Be careful. (Of course, if she is away at school, she hasn't truly left yet.)

You are now an observer of the child you have nurtured and guided. You may make suggestions, if asked. Avoid the urge to make her decisions for her. She can do so. After all, you coached her along the way to help her be a competent decision maker.

A mother not ready to turn loose or trust her absent adult daughter said to her father, "You have to tell her what to do."

The father replied, "She is 25 years old. I do not get to tell her anything. If she wants my advice or suggestion, she has only to ask. But she gets to make his own decisions now."

Enjoy her, continue to love her unconditionally, savor the occasional hugs. The roller-coaster ride is over.

I share with you an excerpted letter I wrote to my son as he was leaving home more than 30 years ago.

My dearest son,

I thought I had told you all I wanted you to know at your graduation, but here I sit on the morning of your departure with something more to say. I have become increasingly sadder with each passing day. This is not the point in time I have relished— the time when you leave home.

I look forward to all that you will accomplish (which I expect will be considerable), but I will share those things from a distance. I like the person you are becoming. I wish you nothing but happy things in your life henceforth. I have tried to prepare you as best I can for what lies ahead.

I will miss you more than you know. I will miss seeing you and hearing about what is going on in your life on a daily basis. I know you will call from time to time and maybe even write a long letter (on your new typewriter?). I will savor those times.

I suppose this is what many call the "empty nest syndrome." The time when the chicks leave the nest to strike out on their own. I don't know how one can prepare for this time, except to say, "It's time."

I want to hold and keep you close, but I know, "It's time." You are capable of doing many things and doing many things well. Keep excellence in focus and set your priorities to accomplish those things that will allow you get what you want ultimately—whatever that is.

I will be as close as the telephone if you need me, but I expect those times of need will be fewer and fewer. That's okay, because it will let me know that you can do what need for yourself. Don't be afraid to ask for help, but don't be afraid to trust yourself either. Just be sure you know which is best—to ask for help or to trust yourself.

I will love you always,
Dad

WHAT COMES NEXT?

If your adolescent has grown into the self-sufficient adult you had hoped, you may be moving into a different role—that of confidant and proud observer of the person you have nurtured. You may anticipate updates on her job and significant other people in her life.

As her life gets busier, you may not hear from her as frequently. It's okay for you to send a note or make a call. Just recognize the seat beside you on the roller coaster is vacant. Again, the roller-coaster ride is over.

FILLING THE VOID

As little as we have prepared to become parents, we are also usually unprepared for not being an active presence in the lives of our children. Even if we still have children at home, there is an empty space our adolescent used to occupy.

We may look back at a frustrating time when we were overwhelmed with parenting and mused about what we would do when the kids were gone. We would have more time for ourselves. We might have more money to spend on ourselves.

The time has come. What can we do with it?

If we have planned thoughtfully, we can execute our plans. If we have left things to serendipity, we wait for life to unfold. The options are constrained only by our energy, imagination, and available funds.

We have more time for practicing hobbies, fixing up our home, volunteering, traveling, and engaging in professional pursuits. We may get the pet we have wanted to supplant the time we spent nurturing our children—or not.

We may think of moving, but to where? Are we place-bound because of our jobs or extended family? Now, we get to choose. Choose wisely.

Survival Tips

- Be prepared to let go.
- See your child as an adult and treat her accordingly.
- Fill the emptying nest thoughtfully.
- Take time for you.

RESOURCE

Parenting and Child Health. (2019). Leaving home: For parents of teenagers and young adults. *Cyh.com.* Available at: http://www.cyh.com/Health Topics/HealthTopicDetails.aspx?p=114&np=122&id=1535, retrieved 14 October 2019.

About the Author

Michael Gilbert, Ed. D., is CEO of ATOIRE Communications, LLC and Professor Emeritus in the College of Education and Human Services at Central Michigan University. He has also been a teacher and administrator in public schools. He has four children and seven grandchildren. Dr. Gilbert is a certified Master Trainer in the Process Communication and Process Education Models. He is also a *Guardian ad Litem*, advocating for youngsters who have been removed from their homes because of abuse, neglect, or violence. He may be reached at atoirecomm@gmail. com, or through http://www.atoire.com.